"GAZED AT IN AWE"

CW00517863

To Derek,

   With best wishes and the hope
that the contents will bring back a
few memories.

[signature]

"GAZED AT IN AWE"

A PERSONAL STORY OF SOLIHULL GAS WORKS AND OF SOME OF THE PEOPLE WHO WORKED THERE

Alan J. Sadler

"The Solihull gas-works, gazed at in awe by a bronchial boy"
W. H. Auden
(Faber & Faber)

BREWIN BOOKS

First published by
Brewin Books, Studley, Warwickshire, B80 7LG
in 1995

ISBN 1 85858 066 8

British Library Cataloguing in Publication Data
A Catalogue record for this book is available from the British Library

Typeset in Times by Avon Dataset Ltd, Bidford on Avon, Warks, B50 4JH
Printed in Great Britain by Alden Press, Osney Mead, Oxford

Acknowledgements

I would like to acknowledge with grateful thanks all the help that has been given to me by the following people. They have helped stir my memory, confirmed various facts or supplied photographs, and given me pleasure in meeting and talking to them. In particluar I appreciated the considerable help I received from Ernie Marshall and Dom O'Donell, who have, I was sad to learn, both since died.

Mr Patrick Ainsworth (son of Mr Ainsworth – Manager 1902–1921)

Mrs Jan Beaseley, Former Librarian to British Gas, West Midlands

Mr Stanley J Beavan, son of Joe Beavan, a long-serving employee of Solihull Gas Company

Mrs Edith Biddle (daughter of Jim Cotton, the Blacksmith)

Mr Jim Cliffe (a gas fitter for Solihull Gas Company from 1938 to its closure in 1962 and then for West Midlands Gas Board until his retirement in 1975)

Mrs May Denton (daughter of Bill Corbett)

Mr Dom O'Donnell (worked for Solihull Gas Company from 1940–45)

Mr Gordon Lisley (formerly a Gas Engineer)

Mr Ernie Marshall (worked for Solihull Gas Company from 1934 to its closure in 1962, except for War Service 1939–1945, and then for the Midland Research Station until 1975)

Mrs Joan Pinfold (daughter of Fred Whitehouse who was a long serving employee at Solihull Gas Company, worked at the offices in Mill Lane 1944–54 and later at West Midlands Gas Headquarters, Wharf Lane)

Miss V E Smith (worked in the Accounts Office in the Mill Lane offices of Solihull Gas Company)

The "Solihull News" – formerly the "Warwick County News".

Solihull Metropolitan Borough Council Library, Local Studies Department.

Fig. 1. The author, "born in the shadow of a gasholder", in the arms of his grandfather.

Introduction

I was born in April 1928 and my birthplace was the Manager's House on Solihull Gas Works, Wharf Lane, Solihull. My father was S J (Stan) Sadler, who was the General Manager of the Works, and for the first eleven years of my life I lived at the Manager's House with my father and mother and elder brother, Geoffrey.

Our family moved to Marsh Lane, Solihull in 1939 but I still kept close links with the Works and the Offices for a number of years and heard all the latest news from my father until he retired in 1955.

I had often thought that the history of Solihull Gas Company should be recorded because many people in Solihull had never heard of the Gas Works and were interested to know a little more about it and where it had been situated.

However, it was a chance meeting at the opening of the new Royal Bank of Scotland premises in High Street (formerly the site of Solihull Picture House) that spurred me into recording the history of the Works and the lives of people who were connected with it.

Amongst the guests at the opening of the new Bank were Mr Charles Lines, the historian, and Sue Bates, the Local Studies Librarian at Solihull Library. It was they who suggested to me that there was very little information regarding the Company and the Works. They also pointed out that there are very few people still alive who would have first hand knowledge of the Works.

Both were of the opinion that a historical reminder should be written and who better to write the history than myself, who had been born actually on the Gas Works. (see Fig. 1)

I suppose that having lived in Solihull for 64 years of my life I had a considerable knowledge of "The Village" and its people.

I retired in 1991 and decided I would begin the task of trying to contact former employees of the Gas Company and anyone else who had been closely connected with the Works and, of course, to consult any records that might still exist. Unfortunately, there now seem to be very few old employees still in Solihull able to help with the history but even now I would be very pleased to hear from anyone that I have missed.

Since the original suggestion by Charles Lines and Sue Bates that a history of the Gas Works should be written, a book by Stanley J Beavan called, "Damson By The Pound" has been produced which includes two chapters on "Solihull Gas Works" and I was very pleased to meet Stanley Beavan and talk about those times. Stanley is the son of Joe Beavan who began work for the Gas Company in 1921 as a mains layer and then became a stoker, van driver, gas fitter and finally a meter reader until he retired in 1958.

I must add that I am not a qualified gas engineer, just an architect, so I am hoping that I have been able to describe the technical side of the Works with reasonable accuracy. Fortunately I have been helped by an ex-gas engineer, Gordon Lisley, who has corrected me when my memory has been at fault or my ignorance has been revealed, and I am grateful to him.

I should also like to express my thanks in particular to Ernie Marshall who began work for the Gas Company in 1934 and finally retired in 1975 having worked at the Midland Gas Research Station after the Gas Works closed.

Another very helpful source of information has been Dom O'Donnell who was involved on the Works from 1940 to 1945.

It is sometimes said that one needs to have a little luck in life and if this is so, my greatest luck came right at the start when I was born into the Sadler family, known to all their friends as Stan and Cis Sadler who then lived at the Manager's House on Solihull Gas Works, in Wharf Lane.

My mother was a quiet and very kind person and a wonderful mother, loved by all who knew her, and my father could not have been a finer father to my elder brother, Geoffrey, and myself.

My father became the driving force in the Gas Company and was in charge of the operational side which grew from a very small Works at the time of his appointment as General Manager in 1921 to a very substantial and successful Company until nationalisation in 1949. He was often called "Mr Gas" in Solihull and was a respected Engineer in the Gas Industry as well as serving as Secretary to the Midland

Association of Gas Engineers and Managers and to the Gas Officers Guild for a number of years.

More important perhaps, he was an excellent "Gaffer" to all the employees on the Works and in the Offices and I am proud that I have received so many tributes to him over the years from past employees.

My father was also very active in helping the community as a whole for almost all the time he lived in Solihull and an announcement of his death in 1963 in the Warwick County News records his many interests. A copy of this announcement concludes this introduction.

This is now the story of Solihull Gas Works gleaned from my own memory and the memories of some of those people who either worked for the Gas Company or who were connected with the Company in some way - information from the few records that are available is also included. I would like the story to be a tribute to my father, S J (Stan) Sadler, for all his work during 34 years of service to Solihull Gas Company and also in recognition of all the men and women who were employed by the Company during its 93 years history. Many of the men worked in hard and unpleasant conditions but there always seemed to be a "family" atmosphere and everyone was a member of a loyal team.

Death of Mr. Stan Sadler: Many local interests

THE death occurred on Saturday of Mr. Stanley James Sadler, who was for more than 30 years general manager of the Solihull Gas Co. He was 72.

Mr. Sadler, who was seriously injured in a motor accident about two years ago had not been in robust health for some time. He was confined to his bed, however, for only a short time before his death. He was living with his son and daughter-in-law, Mr. and Mrs. Alan Sadler, in Homer Road, Solihull. Formerly he lived with his family for many years in Marsh Lane.

He leaves two sons. His wife, Mrs. "Sis" Sadler, died in March of this year. Mr. Alan Sadler is a local architect and his other son, Mr. Geoffrey Sadler is a chartered accountant living in Sutton Coldfield.

Born and educated in Malton, Yorkshire, Mr. Sadler was apprenticed to the High Wycombe Gas Company in 1906 and, in 1913, became the company's assistant manager. By 1916 he was manager of the Tame Valley Gas Co., and, between then and 1921, he held appointments with the Tame Valley, the Ascot Gas and Electrical Co., and the Spennymore Gas Co.

Mr. Sadler moved to Solihull in 1921 and was appointed engineer and manager of the Solihull Gas Co. He held the post until 1932 when he became general manager and secretary of the company. He continued as manager of the nationalised undertaking until his retirement in 1955.

As a sportsman in his younger days Mr. Sadler excelled at cricket, hockey and swimming. He played hockey and cricket for Minor Counties sides, and was also regarded as an outstanding golfer. He was a member of the North Warwickshire Golf Club.

He was founder president of Solihull Rotary Club and conference secretary for No. 106 District of Rotary for some years.

Mr. Sadler also had associations with the Solihull Old People's Welfare Association (of which he was a founder and a former treasurer); with Solihull Bowling Club as a past president; with the Avenue Bowling Club, a former treasurer; with the Solihull Carnival as one of the organisers before the war; and as a member of Solihull Branch of the British Legion. During the last war he was very active in A.R.P. work in the district.

Mr. Sadler also served on governing bodies of several local schools and, as a Freemason, was member of the Silhill and Murdoch Lodges, and a Past Provincial Grand Officer of Warwickshire.

Through his work in the gas industry he was secretary to the Midland Association of Gas Engineers and Managers for a number of years, and was also secretary to te Gas Officers' Guild.

The funeral service was at Solihull Parish Church on Thursday followed by cremation at Yardley.

(newspaper cutting)

Chapter 1

The early days of gas in Solihull

One of the main problems in recounting the history of Solihull Gas Works has been an almost total lack of documents or written information available regarding the Works. It would appear that with the advent of natural gas in the late 1950's, gas works throughout the country rapidly became redundant and they were demolished quite quickly except for some of the gasholders. Certainly, so far as Solihull is concerned, all the office records and archives seem to have been destroyed.

However, my father did relate that the first recorded meeting regarding gas in Solihull was in 1869 in the rather unlikely setting of the vestry in Solihull Parish Church of St Alphege. A meeting was held to consider an application which had been submitted to the Churchwardens for gas lighting to be installed in the village.

At that time, gas was still only used for lighting as the first gas fires and cookers were not produced until around 1850 and they were not in general use for another twenty years.

The first gas street lighting was introduced in 1813 in London and it was soon afterwards that other gas works started to be built and in 1819 most of the larger cities, including Birmingham, had street lighting in certain areas.

The first Gas Company was the Gas Light and Coke Company which was formed in 1812 and covered almost the whole of London as it was at that time.

However, it was not until 1847 that the Gasworks Clauses Act was passed which provided greater control over gas companies mainly through company dividends which were limited to 10%. Gas companies also had to be authorised before they could build a gas works and lay gas mains and they had to show that there was a need for a gas supply.

Subsequent clauses brought about some limitations on gas prices and gas had to conform to certain lighting standards.

The meeting with the Churchwardens of Solihull was, therefore, the first step in the formation of Solihull Gas Company. The idea must have been well received because the Company was quickly formed in the same year and James Knattram was employed as the 'gas maker' at a rate of 17 shillings per week.

There are no details of the first gas works that was built but a plan of 1880 shows one very small Retort House where the gas was produced and three gasholders, two of which were very small and were probably the original holders. A third larger holder seems to have been built in 1875.

One rather unlikely source of information, the House of Commons, does however give some useful facts about the early days of Solihull Gas Company. This was as a result of a Private Bill passed in Parliament in March 1886.

Evidence at the time confirms that the Company was formed in 1869 as a private company with a share capital of £8,000. One of the original directors and a later Chairman was Mr George Beard who lived at Hillfield Hall from 1861 to 1885.

Land was purchased in Wharf Lane adjoining the canal and the Gas Works was built on this green field site. At that time, gas was only supplied to the village of Solihull which was confined to an area bounded by the High Street, Poplar Road, Warwick Road and New Road.

It can be imagined that the original Directors would not have been very popular if they had built their new Works close to the village because of the smell and smoke associated with gas making. A number of early gas works in this country were built adjoining canals before the coming of the railways as canals were then the easiest means of transport for large quantities of coal.

The Oxford and Birmingham Railway had arrived in the 1850's

and the original Solihull Station was opened in 1852. However, the original station was replaced with a new larger station which was built further away from Blossomfield Road on its present site. This station did not open until the early 1930's and presumably the Goods Yard, which was approached off Streetsbrook Road by the side of the present Fire Station, was built at the same time.

I am, therefore, uncertain of the facilities for off-loading coal waggons in the early days of the Gas Company although later on, all the coal was collected from the new Goods Yard.

In any case, in 1869, the Directors would have had to decide if their source of coal supply would be better coming from the canal or the railway if this were possible. It has to be remembered that quite large quantities of coal were involved and the only means of transport was by horse and cart.

As mentioned earlier, the directors would probably have had some difficulty in persuading local landowners to sell their land for a new smelly and smoky gas works close to the village so in the end the Directors seemed to have had little option but to choose a site next to the canal.

At the time, the Directors probably thought the site was quite well situated because there was an existing wharf, named Solihull Wharf, although they would have had considerable additional expense in laying new large cast iron mains all the way into Solihull village. In later years the Company was also to bear the extra expense of transporting coal from the railway to the Works after delivery by canal became uneconomic.

It would have been interesting in retrospect if the Company had been able to persuade the owner of the land adjoining the railway to sell and build the new Gas Works on what is now Dorchester Road. In due course, Alfred Bird would have complained about the smell at his "Tudor Grange" mansion in nearby Blossomfield Road or more likely he would have built it on another site further away.

It is not quite clear how much of the original land adjoining the canal was bought in the first instance but certainly one large field was purchased and this provided sufficient space for the first Works and room in the future for the Manager's House and expansion for the Works.

Fig. 2. An aerial view of the Gas Works taken in 1935–36

This area of land is clearly shown on the aerial photograph, see Fig 2, which was taken around 1935–36 but by that time the first Works had been replaced and the Manager's House had been built. Part of the original field, however, still remained and the hedge running across and meeting Wharf Lane was the original boundary.

The photograph shows a house, gasholder and other buildings on the opposite side of Wharf Lane but this area of land was bought and developed at a future date.

Wharf Lane had been in existence for many years, possibly being formed when the canal was constructed and a wharf provided for the Solihull area. The Anchor Inn had also been built at the end of the lane alongside the canal. One can only assume that the wharf had been built as so many other wharfs in the early days of canals for the loading and unloading of bulk materials for farming, building and of course coal. Canals were the cheapest means of transport in those days for bulk materials and at Solihull Wharf they would have been unloaded and distributed round the area by horse and cart.

At the time when the new gas works was built, the wharf was owned by a Mrs Briscoe, who may have had connections with the Anchor Inn, and I would be interested to know when the Inn was actually built. The roof of the Inn can be seen in the bottom right corner of the aerial photograph. Fig. 2

The canal, eventually called the Grand Union Canal, was originally the Warwick and Birmingham Canal which was opened in 1800 so this could be the date of the Anchor Inn.

In 1869, there were very few houses between the Warwick Road and the canal except for the odd farmhouse or cottage and the whole area round Lode Lane and Elmdon Heath was farmland. The Anchor Inn was therefore in a very isolated position and the only customers would have been the bargees, men visiting the wharf and a few people working on the farms. The arrival of the Gas Works would certainly have improved trade.

There was a door in the lower part of the Inn gable wall which was built right on the edge of the canal so that the Licensee could pass a glass of beer straight into the hand of the bargee when he tied his barge alongside. See Fig. 3

Be that as it may, coal was brought by barges to the wharf in the early days of Solihull Gas Works to use in the production of coal gas and no doubt everyone concerned partook of his pint or quart of ale from this "bar in the wall".

Fig. 3. The Anchor Inn with the door in the gable wall so that beer could be served to bargees

Chapter 2

The original Works and the first expansion of the Company.

The first Gas Works built in Wharf Lane in 1869 was on a small scale but the installations, which included a Retort House, purification plant and gasholders were to a fairly standard design. Most gas works in this country followed this design and such works, but on a larger scale than Solihull, could produce up to 50 million cubic feet of gas per annum.

In 1885, Solihull Gas Company decided that there was a need to expand their gas mains to adjoining areas and the capital would need to be increased by £7,000 to £15,000 with a new Share issue. This expansion scheme required a Private Bill in Parliament to be passed so in March 1886 the proposed Solihull Gas Bill was heard before a Select Committee in the House of Commons.

Considerable detailed evidence was given by various witnesses which reveals interesting information about Solihull at that time and particularly about the gas services. It was stated that in Solihull itself there were about 340 houses with a population of approximately 1,600 and of this number, 48 residents had objected to the expansion scheme of the Company although Counsel for the Gas Company did say that some of these 48 gentlemen were now very sorry they had objected.

Only Solihull village itself was supplied with gas at that time and there were 161 consumers together with 49 street lamps which were in the High Street, Poplar Road, Warwick Road, Mill Lane and Drury

Lane. Annual consumption of coal in 1885 was about 660 tons and in the previous year, output was 4,474,500 cubic feet. It was also reported that in 1885, the Company made a profit of £623 14s 10d. Various experts confirmed that the Gas Works was in good order, in fact in excellent order, and that "very excellent gas" was produced.

It was not stated at the hearing but from other sources it would appear that gas lighting was usually installed in public houses, such as the George Hotel and the Barley Mow and also in the village schools. Gas was supplied to Solihull School from 1881 onwards as well as Lloyds Bank in 1877 and the Public Hall, both of which were in Poplar Road. All these buildings would have been lit by gas together with many of the big houses in the central area.

It would seem certain that the Solihull Workhouse and Solihull Hermitage in Lode Lane would also have had gas lighting because the mains ran past their front doors. I am not sure when gas lighting was installed in St Alphege Church; no doubt somebody will let me know.

Returning to the House of Commons, the main questioning during the hearing seemed to revolve around the relative costs of gas between Birmingham and Solihull. It appears that Solihull Gas Company charged 5s per 10,000 cubic feet whereas Birmingham charged only 2s 6d. Consumer witnesses in the Solihull area seemed to agree that they would rather pay 5s than have no gas at all.

One of the reasons for the higher price in Solihull seemed to be that the isolated position of the Works meant more capital expenditure in laying mains. In addition all the coal had to be transported by horse and cart from the railway, a distance of 1½ miles. Even at that early date, delivery of coal by barge and canal had reduced or ceased altogether.

Presumably, it was cheaper to bring coal direct by rail from Eckington Colliery in Derbyshire, to Solihull Station, and then use a horse and cart to take it to Wharf Lane, Eckington perhaps not being on the canal system. Incidentally, the Committee was told that only the best gas coal was used and this was from Eckington Colliery.

It appeared that the houses in Olton, population given as 936, had gas at that time supplied from Birmingham and no gas was available in Shirley, where there were 200 houses, nor in Blossom Field, said to have 30–40 houses. Knowle had its own gas works on a site in Station Road, now occupied by Evesons Fuels.

It was suggested that the greater Solihull area had about 6,500 inhabitants and the Company considered that there was a demand for gas and a larger number of consumers would mean the operation would be more economical. One of the interested parties was the Vicar of Shirley, Mr Burd, who was a witness and he particularly wanted gas to be made available in Shirley.

At that time, the Manager at Solihull Gas Works was Mr Thomas Burrowes who took the position in 1882 having previously been Manager at Knowle Gas Works. The Solicitor and Secretary to the Company was Mr Richard Sale and Mr Orford Smith, a previous Secretary, was another partner in the Company.

Mr W Dugdale, Q.C. and Counsel for the objectors, accused the Solihull Gas Company of being "nothing more than a company of private adventurers" but this accusation appears to have been totally unjustified as the Works had been well run and was in excellent order. The Directors at that time had never drawn any fees and in fact seemed to be more concerned in giving a public service than making money for themselves.

The Company had already agreed that a new Purifier would have to be provided if the Works was extended and presumably these were the eight "beds" which then remained in use until 1937.

The Select Committee must have agreed with the views of the Gas Company because the Bill and expansion scheme were passed subject only to one condition which stated that the price of gas should not exceed 4s 6d per 1,000 cubic feet. This figure was similar to other gas prices in the country at that time which ranged from 4s 6d to 5s 0d.

This decision meant that the Directors could now proceed with enlargements to the Works and extensions to the gas mains so that gas could be supplied to Shirley and later on to Olton. Provision was thus made for future developments which were to take place in Solihull and the surrounding areas such as Elmdon Heath.

The central area of Solihull was expanding. New shops and roads were being constructed and developed including Ashleigh Road, The Crescent and later Silhill Hall Road and Broad Oaks Road. In addition, new houses were also being built along existing roads such as Streetsbrook Road, Lode Lane, Blossomfield Road, Sharmans Cross Road, Hampton Lane and Warwick Road.

Gas had become a growth industry and Solihull was following the national trend. All this meant that improvements and enlargements would have to be carried out at Wharf Lane.

Chapter 3

Solihull Gas Works 1886–1901

Unfortunately I can find no records to confirm when the first major rebuilding of the Works took place but it must have begun soon after the Private Bill had been passed. The architectural style of the buildings indicates that the building was constructed towards the end of the century and I am assuming therefore that the whole of the Works was virtually re-built between 1890 and 1900.

The rapid expansion of Solihull also meant that gas production would have had to increase. The original Works could not have met these demands.

I had hoped that the Ordnance Survey Maps would have helped to confirm the dates but this has not been so. The 1880 Edition shows the original Works with a very small Retort House and three gasholders and the wharf described as "Solihull Wharf". The next Ordnance Survey Map of 1917 which was surveyed in 1913–1914 still shows the small Retort House but no gasholders at all and the wharf is no longer named.

I can only think that the draughtsman must have had a little doze at the time because I am sure all the new buildings would have been completed at that time and certainly there would have been gasholders in existence. Ordnance plans are usually very accurate but this was in the early days. At least the buildings are shown accurately on the 1952 Edition.

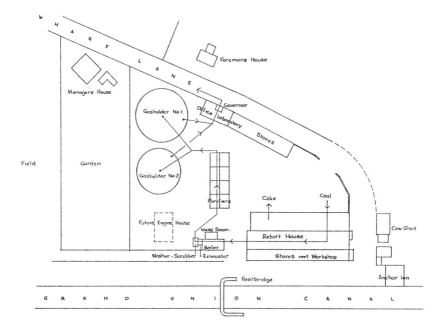

*Fig. 4. A plan of Solihull Gas Works,
typical of a small works at the turn of the century*

The layout of the gas works followed closely a typical design for a small works at the turn of the century. See Fig. 4

All the buildings at the turn of the century are also clearly shown on the aerial photograph. See Fig. 2

The Works was confined to the left hand side of Wharf Lane. The larger gasholder and house and garden on the opposite side of the Lane were built later.

Coming down Wharf Lane, the first building after the large gasholder was the original office building, (see also Fig. 5), consisting of three rooms with a chemist's laboratory added on at the end. These rooms all had fireplaces, with gas fires of course.

In this first building, the one room was used as the Manager's Office, another room was the General Office with one clerk and in between was the Entrance Hall which had in the middle what looked to me like a very small gasholder, possibly five feet in diameter, which I am told was a "governor", but more about that later.

The next buildings with lean-to roofs running along the lane were used for storage of all sorts of pipes and fittings. Then can be seen the main gateway with very high walls on either side and tall iron gates. The gateway led into the main yard area where coal was stored ready to be used in the Retort House which was the very large building next to the Yard. A large chimney can be seen at the end of the Retort House and air vents can be seen in the roof from which the fumes escaped.

Between the Retort House and the canal is another line of buildings which were used for a variety of purposes, i.e. storage, the mechanic's workshop, washrooms, etc. To the left of these buildings is another pitched roof building with a very high chimney. This building contained a large steam boiler which in the early days provided all the power needed to run the Works.

Below the Boiler House can be seen the footbridge but there is no record when it was built. However this bridge proved a very useful link when Elmdon Heath began to develop because people were then able to walk along the tow path and cross the bridge to reach the

Fig. 5. The gasholder which was built at the turn of the century with the original office building in the centre. The photograph was taken just before the gasholder and all the buildings were demolished in 1962.

Anchor Inn. Quite a number of the Works employees also lived in Elmdon Heath so walking alongside the canal was a much shorter and more pleasant journey than by road.

The wharf can be seen to the right of the bridge and the roof of the Anchor Inn is just visible in the corner. The small building behind the Boiler House was the workers' Mess Room or Canteen. As a small boy, I was often asked into the Mess Room by the stokers and at first I was rather wary because they were a ragged group of men, very dirty and often covered in sweat having come from the appalling conditions of the Retort House. It was a gloomy room with dirty windows and dark green painted walls.

However, I soon found out that without exception they were tough but kind men and I would be offered a large metal mug of tea. The tea was usually very strong so I was not too keen but the bacon and eggs with fried bread from the frying pan on the red hot coke stove were always very welcome. We all sat down on long wooden benches and enjoyed the feast.

Adjoining the Boiler House, was the tall "Washer" plant which helped to clean impurities from the raw gas. The pitched roofed building behind the "Washer" plant was the Engine House but this was added at a later date because of the need for electricity on the Works.

As I mentioned earlier, I think the smaller of the two gasholders would have been one of the early holders and was probably built in 1875 with the second larger holder added when the rest of the Works was re-built.

The eight low rectangles adjoining the gasholders in the open yard were the "purifier beds". Each one was built with brick perimeter walls about four feet high and each "bed" was approximately twenty feet by twelve feet and covered with a large and very heavy steel "lid". The purifier beds were the final stage in removing the last of the impurities from the gas.

So how was gas produced initially from coal and what were the various stages in its preparation before it was ready to be distributed to the consumers in Solihull?

14

Chapter 4

How gas was produced.

The production of gas was first carried out in this country by William Murdoch (1754–1839) around 1792 and his experiments with gas for lighting were continued in Birmingham at the Soho Works of Boulton and Watt at the turn of the century.

I will not go into too many technical details because I am not qualified but I hope that I will be able to give the basic methods of gas production and how it operated in Solihull.

Murdoch first of all discovered that a combustible gas was given off when coal was heated, a process called carbonisation, and in the first instance, after certain purification, this gas was used for lighting only. Gas fires and cookers came on the scene at a much later date.

It was found that the quality of the gas coal was very important and so was the temperature at which the coal was heated or "baked". Coal was first baked in cast iron retorts and later, in about 1866, horizontal retorts which were lined with fire bricks were introduced and this method of producing gas did not basically change until the advent of natural gas in 1949. The design of the retorts was improved and vertical retorts were found to be more efficient but the traditional process of making gas from coal remained the same.

Having decided on a colliery who could supply high quality gas coal, and a means of transport to the Gas Works, Solihull Gas Company began the first steps in gas production. The gas coal, having been emptied from the barges at the canal wharf, was loaded on to a cart and pulled by a horse to the Yard adjoining the Retort House. I am not sure what type of cart was used first of all but later on I remember seeing that it had a "tipping" arrangement so that it was easy to unload.

It also appears that in the early days the Company paid for this work to be done and even in the 1920's Mr Raven, the licensee of the Anchor Inn, supplied the horse and cart and also the man for the task of moving the coal from the wharf to the coal yard.

The coal was taken into the Retort House by wheelbarrow and placed on the floor ready to be loaded into the retorts.

The first Retort House was only a small installation but later on, between 1890 and 1900, a much larger Retort House was built and this remained in production until 1937 and was not demolished for many years. It was a dark cavernous building, the only light coming in from the space round the air vents in the roof and the door openings in one side of the building.

There were gas lights high in the roof to give additional light because production never stopped night or day but even so the men worked in semi-darkness because there was little reflected light as everywhere was covered in black carbon from the smoke. As a small boy, I always thought it was like walking into Dante's Inferno when the retorts were being loaded or unloaded.

There was a massive structure inside which stretched for almost the full length of the building and within this structure were set the "retorts". The retorts were really ovens in which the coal was baked. The retorts were rather like long tubes but 'D' shaped in section with the flat part at the bottom and they were built in fireclay or silica bricks.

The retorts were grouped together, I forget how many but probably four or six, and these groups, called "banks", were repeated down the length of the Retort House, rather like a row of bakery ovens, each "bank" being about ten feet wide. There were probably eight "banks". The whole structure was built in brickwork and the tunnel shaped retorts extended the full depth of the structure, almost twenty feet. Each retort could be opened at either end by means of cast iron doors rather like those seen on railway steam engines.

Below the banks of retorts were the furnaces or "producers" which provided the hot gases which were circulated round the retorts via flues. The fuel used to create these extremely hot gases was coke which was red hot, mixed with a lean gas, called the producer gas, which was mainly carbon monoxide, hydrogen and inert nitrogen.

In the early days of Retort Houses, the stokers had to shovel all the coal by hand into the retorts at one end, again rather like railway firemen who always had to have an accurate throw through a small opening. Originally the stokers had to shovel the coal which had been left in heaps on the floor by labourers from their wheelbarrows. This was no mean task as tons of coal were being put through the retorts at any one time.

As the coal was loaded into the retorts, other men had to push the coal down the length of the retort tunnel with very long handled tools called "rams" and then level it off. I am not sure how much coal was shovelled into each retort but I would think possibly half a ton. The coal had to be levelled off to provide a space of about four inches between the top of the coal and the top of the retort. This gap allowed the gas which was given off to pass along the retort.

The doors at either end of each retort were then shut and the process of extracting gas from the coal began. The temperature in the one bank of retorts was then raised so that the coal in the retorts began to fuse and the gas started to be given off, as with a bottle of lemonade, and rose to the top of the retorts.

The gas was able to escape from the retorts by way of vertical pipes positioned along the tops of the retorts. These pipes were called ascension pipes and these rose to a high level where they were connected to a collector main which then took the gas away from the Retort House.

During this baking process in the retorts, called carbonisation, the structure of the coal gradually changed to a grey porous material called "coke" – a little difficult to describe but rather like a solid sponge, hard and very rough to the touch. It was honeycomb in texture, similar to the inside of a Crunchie bar.

By the way, the number of retorts that were in action at any one time depended on the need for gas so in the very cold weather, the whole Retort House was in full production. Each bank of retorts was

17

filled in strict rotation and after approximately eight hours the coal would have been 'baked' and all the available gas would have been removed from the retorts. The process of emptying the retorts, or "discharging" then began. This was a very demanding and horrific job.

The discharging process began with opening each of the doors at one end of the retorts. The doors were sealed against iron spigots at the end of each retort and the doors had a two stage opening action with a long metal handle to operate it. When the retort was ready to have the coke removed, the first movement of the handle would be made. This would allow some gas to escape which was then ignited by the stoker with a burning taper or a piece of tarred rope which had been lit.

Depending on how completely the gas had been extracted from the coal, this would give a flame about a foot high. Next the handle would be fully opened and the door opened when, depending on the completion of the extraction of gas from the coal, the flame could reach up to the roof, especially after several doors had been opened.

The alternative way of opening a retort was much more spectacular. It was usually reserved for occasions when visitors were present, but deprecated by the management because it could damage the "setting" – the brickwork forming the retorts and the supporting structure. This way was to ignore the first stage of door opening procedure and just fling the door open. Unlit gas would then pour upwards from the retort towards the roof and when it had mixed with sufficient air, two or three seconds later, ignite with a loud boom.

This muffled explosion would impress or frighten the visitors with both the noise and flash ignition followed by clouds of carbon dust from the roof members, that is if the trick had not been done recently. Sparks were also given off and these spectacular performances by the stokers concluded with the large flame continuing to burn roofwards from the mouth of the retort.

The retort men were then heroes in the eyes of the beholders, which definitely did not include the management, but the stokers were largely a good natured band of workers and the management relied on them to keep supplies of gas going at peak times in very bad conditions so there was a certain amount of "not noticing" although the loud booms could be heard some distance away.

The doors at the other ends of the retorts would then be opened by other men and the remainder of the red hot coke would be pulled out with the rakes or "drag bars" as they were called. Even if the doors were opened properly and the stokers behaved themselves, the heat and fumes were intense and the men had to get out of the way very quickly when the retorts were exposed.

The coke would pile up in front of the retorts when it was raked out at the discharge end and it would then have to be dowsed with water to cool it off and large amounts of steam would be given off. The coke at this stage would be in large lumps fused together but when cooled, it was easier to handle.

As the gas rose up the ascension pipes, the vapours in the gas began to condense in the pipes. Because of the heat of the gas, the gas vapours would form a hard carboniferous tarry lining to the pipes. I cannot remember but I am told that these pipes then had to be kept clean by men with long bent rods of metal about 20 feet long with a handle at one end and an auger head at the other. The auger heads were forced up the pipes from the retort end by manual effort to clear away the tarry lining. This task was a most arduous, unpleasant, smelly and hot job and the men could only work for a few minutes before taking a rest, such were the conditions.

You will now begin to realise why I thought the inside of the Retort House was like Dante's Inferno. The inside of the building and everything in it, including the men, was covered in coal and carbon dust, the air was full of smoke and acid fumes, the heat was intense and steam was continually being given off from the quenched coke.

The conditions were dreadful, and sometimes dangerous, as were many industrial factories in the Victorian era. The gas works did not change much after that time and gas making was very demanding for the stokers and labourers shovelling coal and then raking out the red hot retorts. The temperature in the building would be very hot but there would be intervals between the retorts being opened when icy winds would blow in winter time through the open side of the building.

The men who worked in the Retort House usually seemed to be well wrapped up with heavy shirts and woollen vests, thick trousers and of course they all wore heavy boots or clogs with steel tips. One minute they would be covered in sweat and shortly after they could be in an icy draught so they had to cater for all conditions.

Because of the need to keep the gasholders and mains full, gas had to be produced almost every hour of the day and every day of the year. Work rarely stopped and stokers and labourers worked in shifts, either 8 or 12 hours at a time, day and night and particularly at Christmas time when demand for gas was at a peak.

Life improved a little soon after my father became manager in 1921 when a mechanical stoking machine, or charging machine as it was sometimes called, was installed. This machine ran up and down the Retort House on rails in front of the retorts and automatically charged the retorts with coal and could discharge the coke from the one end. The machine was electrically powered and the manual effort was considerably reduced.

When night shifts were worked, some relatives would bring their men supper in the evenings. One lady, Mrs Edith Biddle, the daughter of Jim Cotton who was the blacksmith in Damson Lane, has told me that Jack Larner, one of the stokers, used to live next door to them. During the summer evenings, when Jack was on night shift, his wife and son together with Edith, would walk along the canal tow path from Damson Lane to the little footbridge opposite the Works where they crossed over and went in to give Jack his supper. Edith was then given rides on the charging machine up and down the Retort House when the retorts were not being charged.

The stokers and labourers were not working continuously for the eight or twelve hour shifts. They had breaks between each "draw" of the retorts but when the pressure was on, they worked very hard indeed and the element of danger was always there.

It has been said that working in a Retort House on a gas works soon made old men out of young ones. Because of the excessive heat, fumes and very hard work, the men had to drink a lot to avoid dehydration. Drinks ranged from tea to beer, both in copious amounts and also milk was valued for medical reasons though this value is now discredited.

So far as I am aware, there were no proper washing facilities except for the odd basin or sink in the lavatory and showers were unknown. I query if there was any hot water in the early days other than from the kettle in the Mess Room. Life was very spartan and the advent of "Ascot" water heaters must have come as a very welcome relief. It will also be appreciated that the Anchor Inn, only a few yards away from the Retort House, was a very popular spot to go at the end of the day or shift.

Just before we return to the gas production process, a word about the coke which had been removed from the retorts. Many younger people and even some of middle age have never seen or heard of coke. In fact it was possibly the first of the smokeless fuels; an accidental discovery from a by-product of gas production.

As the gas works became more mechanised, the coke, once it had been cooled, was taken by overhead crane to a very large revolving cylinder supported at high level by a steel structure which can be seen on the aerial photograph in the open yard behind the Retort House. The coke was broken up and graded by the cylinder which had perforations of various sizes.

The pieces of coke which dropped through the holes were very uneven in shape and rough but they were graded as three inch (75mm), and various sizes down to the smallest size called "breeze" which was about 3/4 inch (19mm). The cylinder dropped the different sized coke into hoppers which were positioned with the bottoms about four or five feet above the yard level, so that bags, carts or lorries could be positioned underneath. A lever would then be pulled and coke of the required size would be dropped into the waiting receptacle. The "bagging up" of the coke in my younger days was in the hands of "Oily Bill" Whitehouse who ruled his little operation with a very firm hand. It appears that he gained his nickname because he used to fill oil lamps and always smelt of oil.

Coke was sold to individual customers and also to commercial users. In the Victorian era and later, the air in the bigger cities was very polluted and smoke from coal fires and other coal appliances contributed very much to the pollution. Coke was therefore welcomed as a smokeless fuel and it was used extensively in boilers and stoves of all types both in industry and in the home. Small heating stoves and domestic boilers usually used "breeze", the smallest size available. Coke gave off an intense heat and was very light and easy to handle.

Even the coke dust or ash as it was called, was sold for a variety of purposes. A thick layer of ash was often laid under lawns and other surfaces to help drain these areas. It was also used as a temporary surface for roads and sometimes a permanent finish for footpaths because it drained well and was quite hard-wearing when consolidated. The footpath leading from Cornyx Lane across School Lane to the village alongside Solihull School playing fields was covered with ash and was always known as the "cinder path"; no doubt the ash came from the Gas Works. Every by-product in gas making had a use and nothing was ever wasted. In the early days, coke and ash were taken away from the Works by horse and cart, later by lorry. Coke and ash were also loaded on to the canal barges and then transported to factories in the Midlands.

Returning to the gas making process, mention should be made that the spent hot gases that had circulated round the retorts and kept them white hot were eventually collected in the flues and dispersed out of the large chimney.

The collector main at high level sloped down towards one end of the Retort House. As the gas cooled in the collector main, condensation took place and the liquid formed contained ammonia with globules of tar. This ammoniacal liquor ran down the collector main to the end where it was collected in a tank and the tar separated out.

It was considered by many people that being able to breathe the fumes from the tar tank helped those suffering from chest complaints such as asthma, whooping cough and bronchitis and quite a number of people, usually children with their parents, would come at the week-ends or in the evenings to clear their lungs. They would lean over the edge of the steel tank and breathe in the tar fumes, in other words it was a coal tar remedy.

I have heard from one lady, one of three children in her family, who suffered from whooping cough in the early 1920's, and she was taken to the Works to breathe in the coal tar fumes. It appears that Mr Kennard, the Foreman, gave the mother three short lengths of rope soaked in tar and the mother went home, made three bags with the rope inside and then tied the bags round the children's necks so that they could breathe in the fumes all the time – the forerunner to vaporisers! The poet, W H Auden, was also taken on the 7 mile journey from his family home in Harborne, Birmingham, to Solihull Gas

Works to help cure his bronchitis. He describes the visit in his poem – Prologue at 60 – "the Solihull gas-works, gazed at in awe by a bronchial boy" – the source for the title of this book.

The tar which was a thick black oily liquid, was taken away by barge for various uses in industry as well as road construction and the production of creosote which was used in huge quantities for preservation of railway sleepers.

The ammoniacal liquor, which was filtered off, was sold off for spraying on fields or conversion to ammonium sulphate which is another fertiliser. All these by-products from gas production provided the Gas Company with useful income and we forget that all these valuable natural materials are no longer available since the advent of natural gas and coal gas production ceased.

Meanwhile, the partially purified gas was being passed through an overhead pipe to the Washer Plant which was the tall structure just behind the Boiler House chimney. I will not attempt to try to explain how this "washing" process worked, suffice it to say that it further cooled the gas and removed the last of the condensates.

Another item of equipment was the "Exhauster" which was a steam driven pump which drove the gas from the Retort House through the Washer and on to the Purifier Beds. I am told that these pumps were extremely reliable, which they had to be because they were expected to work 24 hours per day and 365 days per year. Steam also had the advantage of not causing any sparks which could happen with electricity with possibly an explosive result if there were a gas leak nearby.

In any case, there was no electricity on the Works until the 1920's so up to that time all lighting was by gas and the exhauster, pumps, etc. were all steam driven. The large boiler in the Boiler House provided all the necessary steam.

After the first washing processes, the gas was further purified in the iron oxide "beds" which can be seen as the eight large rectangular shapes by the side of the two gasholders. Purifier beds were always kept well away from the Retort House because of the fire risk.

These enclosed purifier beds were built above ground level with large removable steel lids which were lifted off in turn by the crane that ran along the tracks between the beds and could carry two of the lids at a time, one on either side.

In each bed, there were two or three tiers of timber racks with open grids. Iron oxide, which was a peat-like material and rust coloured, was placed on the timber grids where the gas was passed through the iron oxide and various chemical changes then took place. The original quite pleasant material became hard and clogged with tarry, gummy deposits from the gas and the sulphurous materials from the gas, mostly hydrogen sulphide.

I always knew that whenever the lids were lifted off there was a very nasty smell just like "bad eggs" and I have put down my present poor sense of smell to those years of living so close to the beds. The smell came from the hydrogen sulphide which caused the iron oxide to change to iron sulphide. As soon as a bed of iron oxide had absorbed all the impurifications it had to be changed and this involved the removal of the lids and clearing out the particular beds. The changing of the material had to be done in strict rotation but it was a dangerous task and there was always the risk of fire.

All the valves had to be turned off, wooden mallets being used to loosen the metal fittings on the lids and nothing was done to create a spark. I often think about the appalling conditions in which those men had to work when they cleaned out and recharged the beds by breaking up the material with picks and then shovelling it over the sides into a wheelbarrow or lorry.

The spent iron oxide was then taken to the far side of Wharf Lane and dumped in heaps which can be seen by the side of the third gasholder. This material was grey/green in colour and I understand that when left out in the open, it gradually absorbed oxygen from the atmosphere and reverted to iron oxide. The iron oxide was then taken back to the beds and in this way was used a number of times to get the best value from it – one of the early re-cycling operations.

Not all the smell was removed from the purified gas so that if leaks did occur anywhere, particularly in customers' homes or other buildings, it would be easily noticed. Similarly, natural gas used today has an additive which creates a smell, essential in detecting leaks. When the iron oxide was completely spent, it was then sold to chemical manufacturers who extracted the sulphur element, a quite valuable chemical for all sorts of products.

After the gas had been finally purified, it was fed by underground pipes to the gasholders for storage. Gasholders are often incorrectly described as gasometers but a gasometer is an instrument for measuring the volume of gas – gasholder is the correct term. The early gasholders were big steel cylinders with a slightly domed top but open at the bottom. They were made of steel plates, riveted together rather like a ship's hull and were of the single lift type. Another cylinder with a slightly larger diameter, but with a bottom and no top, was set in the ground and the upper cylinder was then put inside the lower one.

The lower cylinder was filled with water to form a seal so as the gas was let in, the upper cylinder was gradually lifted up by the gas with the water seal preventing any escape of gas. The upper cylinder was about two feet less in diameter than the lower one so you could always see a channel of water between them, about 9 – 12 inches wide – just below the top of the lower cylinder or ground level.

The first two small gasholders at Solihull were only about 30 feet in diameter but a third larger holder, possibly built around 1875–1880 had a diameter of between fifty and sixty feet. This holder, the smallest on the aerial photograph, had two cylinders showing above ground level which slid inside each other, rather like a telescope except that the upper section had a channel round the bottom outer edge and the lower section lipped over it. There was water in the channel so again there was a water seal to prevent gas escaping. The channels were two to three feet deep.

The two sections which were above ground level then moved up and down depending on the amount of gas fed into them. The two heavy steel cylinders had cast-iron steel columns spaced round the perimeter and there were rollers between the cylinders and the columns so they would rise and lower quite smoothly. This type was called a vertical frame rise and fall holder.

Some of the earlier gasholders without supporting columns did tip or collapse. In 1884 one of the small holders of this type at Solihull blew down as the result of a severe storm. Considerable damage was also done to other buildings on the Works.

Gas works always had at least two holders because if there was a problem with one holder and it was the only one, there would be no gas and with no pressure, air could enter the mains creating a serious risk of explosion in properties.

As production of gas increased at Solihull, so did the need for additional storage and a further larger gasholder was built alongside the other one and close to the Manager's House. This holder was about 50 feet high and 60 – 70 feet in diameter and it can be seen on the photographs, Figs 2 and 3, as a three lift type. In later years two even larger holders were to be built but although the sections of the holders were so heavy and massive, their design and operation were so simple that as the gas was fed into them, they would rise gradually as the pressure increased and then lower smoothly as the gas was drawn off.

Besides storage, the gasholders served another purpose which was to create the required pressure on the gas so it could be safely distributed throughout Solihull, the massive weight of the cylinders pressing down all the time on the gas which was being stored in the holders.

On Christmas Day, particularly if the weather was very cold, the holders would get very low as a lot of gas would be used but of course in summer when demand was less they would often be full. It was then that the Manager or Foreman had to check how much gas was being produced because if the pressure of gas being pumped in was too great, the holder could get over full and blow out under the lowest section.

My father, when he was at home and not in the office in Mill Lane, would always be looking out of the window, particularly during the winter to check that sufficient gas was available. This was of course the whole art – to keep enough gas in the holders to give an even supply and the retorts kept going to replenish them at peak times.

Nowadays it is the electricity generating stations who have to check on "peak demands" often depending on a particular television programme. At the Gas Works, the demand for gas was ruled by the need for heat and cooking and later on, the requirements of industry.

Before gas was allowed into the gas mains supplying Solihull, it was taken underground from the gasholders to the "governor" in the office building and close to the chemist's laboratory. I have been told that the governor ensured that the gas leaving the Works was at the correct pressure which by law the Company had to maintain, neither too low nor too high.

The original gas main ran under Wharf Lane, Hermitage Lane and Lode Lane to the village, but later all these mains had to be considerably enlarged and a complete new network laid to a very much larger area.

Throughout the gas production process, the chemist would check the quality and purity of the gas and the various processes which took place. I can only remember that Mr Whitehouse was the chemist during the 1930's and probably after that but his work was obviously very important to ensure that the purity and the calorific value of the gas were correct.

It can therefore be seen that it was logical for the Manager and Chemist to be close to each other, and to the "governor", in case of any serious problem.

Such was the method of gas production in the early days of Solihull Gas Works and little altered until the 1930's.

Chapter 5

Changes to Solihull Gas Works 1902–1921

In 1902, the Directors appointed Mr Ainsworth as the new Manager and he worked from the small room in the original office building in Wharf Lane.

For a while, Mr and Mrs Ainsworth lived in a small cottage near the Anchor Inn but as their family grew, the Company decided to provide a Manager's House and this would seem to have been built just before the 1914–1918 War. This house was attractively designed, see Fig. 6, and had a high standard of accommodation for that time, including two living rooms, spacious hall, kitchen, scullery, four bedrooms, bathroom, WC, a separate timber wash house and even an outside WC. The house, which was built facing Wharf Lane and immediately adjoining the Works, also had a very large garden stretching down to the canal as can be seen on the aerial photograph and Fig. 7.

The provision of such a pleasant house would have been very welcome to Mr Ainsworth because at that time his working life must have been very difficult. He was obviously heavily engaged with the first expansion of the Works which would have been taking place including the new Retort House, building the new purifier beds, the second gasholder and in due course the third gasholder.

New gas mains had to be laid or enlarged as new areas required to be supplied. I am not sure when Solihull Gas Company took over the

Fig. 6. Our family home – "The Manager's House"

Fig. 7. Part of the garden to the Manager's House

responsibility of providing gas to Olton but it was sometime just before Mr Ainsworth's arrival at the Works so this was another addition to the workload. Street lighting was also to become an expanding area.

It was 1899 that Solihull Rural District Council took over control of street lighting from the Solihull Lighting Inspectors. There was some opposition to the proposed change in authority because objectors thought the Council would spend more than they should on lighting. However, the change took place and the objectors' worst fears were soon proved correct because the Council lost no time in extending their street lighting.

They installed 6 extra lights in Solihull, 30 in Olton and 28 in Shirley together with lighting to other roads during 1902–1903. Lighting was briefly deferred in Blossomfield Road but 30 lamps were in position in 1904. Gas street lamps, as they were called, all had gas mantles fitted which gave an intense white light but in the early years they had to be lit by hand every night and then turned off again in the morning.

It is not surprising therefore that the first signs of competition to Solihull Gas Company came in 1904 when Solihull Council considered changing their street lighting from gas to electricity. Electric street lighting had not really been developed until after the 1914–1918 War. For whatever the reason, Solihull Council decided to keep to gas but an offer by the Gas Company to reduce the cost of gas down to 3d per 1,000 cubic feet was not unconnected.

At some time, the Company must have purchased quite a large area of land on the opposite side of Wharf Lane to the main works, possibly during the time of Mr Ainsworth. It was on this land that further storage buildings were placed and a large weighbridge positioned at the side of the road. The weighbridge was used for checking coal deliveries and to weigh coke and ash that had been sold. These buildings and the weighbridge can be seen on the righthand side of Wharf Lane just in front of the large gasholder. A further small building with a curved roof was added at the rear and this was used for the maintenance section.

The Gas Company was expanding all through the period of 1900–1921, but for Mr Ainsworth, the greatest pressure occurred during the 1914–1918 First World War. Many workers had joined the Services and a great deal of extra work had to be undertaken by Mr Ainsworth and the additional stress and physical work was thought to be the cause of his early death in 1921.

It should not be overlooked that Solihull Gas Company did also have a presence in Solihull village. Records show that Lloyds Bank built new premises for themselves in 1877 in Poplar Road but this building must have been much too large for their own requirements at that time and part of the ground floor premises was let to the Gas Company. Fig. 8.

The offices were only small and presumably were for administration purposes only and for accounts but the Company remained there until about 1919–1920. At that time there was a need for additional office space and the Bank was also expanding and needed the area occupied by the Gas Company.

It was not until just before the turn of the century that the design of gas cookers and fires became practical and running costs more

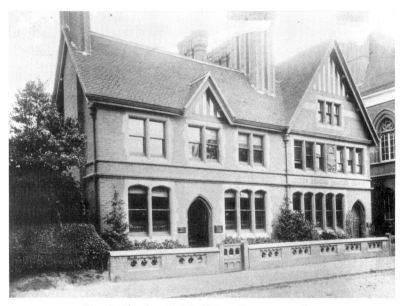

Fig. 8. The first Solihull Gas Company offices
in the Poplar Road premises of Lloyds Bank

competitive compared to coal. As the demand for these appliances increased in the early 1900's so the Gas Company decided that there was a need for a central showroom in Solihull village. Besides additional office space, there was also the need for premises for gas fitters and meter readers who needed to be on the same site.

Fortunately, a suitable building and site were found in Mill Lane and, by coincidence, the present British Gas showroom in Mill Lane stands on the original site. The purchase took place about 1919–1920.

The buildings and site which the Directors purchased were ideal for the new use. Their good foresight was confirmed in later years because it remained in use with only minor alterations until the central area of Solihull was largely demolished and re-built as Mell Square in the early 1960's.

In those days, walking down Mill Lane from High Street, the first building on the left was the bakery of Mr Davis which was behind his shop in the High Street. Shortly after the bakery was a row of

Fig. 9. The Gas Offices and Showroom, still in Mill Lane in the 1950's, can be seen as the three-storey building left of centre.

33

cottages followed by the building which was to become the main offices and showroom of the Gas Company.

The main building which came to the back of the pavement, was three storeys in height, domestic in character, with a single width driveway on the right followed by another row of cottages. The driveway led to a large yard at the rear where there were a number of outbuildings and a large two storey building with a flat roof.

It has been suggested that the main building at the front, which I think would have been built in the early 1900's, was originally used as a telephone exchange. I am doubtful if this was the case but I would be interested to hear from anyone who may know.

I do know, however, that the premises were occupied by Saxtree and Bullivant, who were Bakers and Confectioners, and I would think it more likely that the premises were built for them originally, particularly as there was a purpose built shop incorporated in the original design. This shop covered half the frontage and was to become the future gas showroom.

The large two-storey building at the back of the yard had been used as a bakery and in later years I am told that it was also a place where children from the school in Park Road were given cookery classes. One of the pupils of those days was Nancy Davies. She remembers that pupils went in groups to Mill Lane to be taught how to use gas cookers. She left this school in 1925.

Another lady, Mrs Edith Biddle (née Cotton) said she also went to this building for cookery classes a few years later so the Gas Company must have helped out the school in this way. The gas fitters' store was on the ground floor but there was a separate staircase to the room above so the girls would have had easy access.

After Saxtree and Bullivant, and before the purchase by the Gas Company, the premises were occupied by Mr A J Bayliss and his family. Mr Bayliss later built his garage and showroom for Morris cars on the Warwick Road opposite to the other end of Mill Lane. Miss Ida Bayliss, the daughter of Mr A J Bayliss, told me that the building at the front became their family home. The large shop window was covered over so that their surplus furniture could be stored in the area behind, previously the shop. In 1919–1920 the Bayliss's then sold the buildings and yard to Solihull Gas Company. The old shop

34

area became the new showroom and the first floor rooms together with one room on the ground floor, were used as offices. The buildings leading off the Yard at the back became Stores used by the gas fitters and meter readers.

It was just after this development for the Company that Mr Ainsworth died. No doubt in those days there would have been little or no pension for Mr Ainsworth, particularly as he died at a relatively young age and it was therefore pleasing to learn from one of his sons that the Directors gave the use of the spacious top floor of the building in Mill Lane to Mrs Ainsworth and her children where they remained until the early 1930's. It appears the accommodation for the family was provided rent free and this benevolent action of the Company seems to be very much part of their history and records show this attitude followed a similar paternalism throughout the gas industry.

Chapter 6

The years of major expansion – 1921–1939

In 1921 my father, S J Sadler, usually known as Stan, was appointed as Mr Ainsworth's successor. My father began as a pupil in the gas industry in 1906 and then graduated as a Gas Engineer with posts in High Wycombe, Tame Valley, Ascot and Spennymoor. He and my mother, Cis Sadler, came to Solihull in 1921 just after they were married. Both were natives of Yorkshire and both had been born in Malton in the East Riding.

At that time, Solihull Gas Company was still a private company with Directors and Shareholders and remained so until it was nationalised in 1949. The Gas Works still stood in complete isolation at the end of Wharf Lane but not for long because it was about this time, in the early 1920's that houses and shops began to be built in Elmdon Heath. The majority of all these new houses were Council built and they provided homes for quite a number of the gas workers and their families.

At the time of his appointment, I am sure the Directors told my father that Solihull was a growing area and there would be an excellent future for him and so it proved to be. Solihull had almost doubled its size from the 10,000 inhabitants that there were in 1911 and in 1932 when Solihull was to become an Urban District Council, the population was recorded as 25,000. Who would have imagined in 1921 that in 1954, towards the end of the Gas Works era, that the population would be 72,000? Probably even the Directors of Solihull Gas Company would not have forecast that level of expansion.

I can find no record of developments at the Gas Works during the 1920's but two major improvements took place sometime during that period. It was obviously decided that an electricity supply would have to be made available on the Works, particularly for the new stoking machine. The advent of electricity on a gas works was quite an event but I am sure there would have been no main cables in the area so the Directors took a sensible decision – the purchase of a gas engine which produced electricity as and when required.

The engine and its equipment were quite large so a new Engine House had to be built and this can again be seen on the aerial photograph as the pitched roofed building with two roof cowls between the Boiler House chimney and the bottom of our garden. The building had large windows all the way round and was spotlessly clean with red tiles on the floor and green painted walls.

Gas engines were the first of the internal combustion engines and as their efficiency improved were found to be very reliable and economic. Reliability was very important bearing in mind that the power it supplied had to be available every hour and every day of the year. They were economic because they used the gas produced on the Works and although the engine had to be available at all times, it was only in action as and when electricity was required for the various equipment it supplied.

The machinery inside the Engine House was well spaced out but the whole area was dominated by the huge flywheel, eight to nine feet in diameter. There was a large pit into which the lower part of the wheel was recessed and the whole area was railed off to prevent possible accidents when the wheel was spinning at considerable speed.

The whole set-up was very impressive and was obviously a great asset to the efficient running of more up-to-date electric powered equipment which was being installed. The Engine House even had its own electric lighting, the first and I think the only building on the Works to have such lighting until 1938 and even then all the old buildings and offices continued to use gas lighting for a number of years after that time.

The other major addition to the Works was the erection of a third gasholder which was built on the opposite side of Wharf Lane to the other two holders. This additional gasholder was a three lift type, very much larger than the others, and would have more than doubled the storage capacity for gas on the Works. Demand for gas was increasing all the time.

Such was the Gas Works in the 1920's and further afield in the district, new and larger gas mains were being laid to the ever growing built up areas.

So it was in 1926 that my brother Geoffrey was born and then in April 1928, my birth took place in our house at the side of the Works, Dr Whitehouse and Nurse Gloster were in attendance. For the first three years of my life I was not really aware that I lived in a rather

Fig. 10. The author at work and play

unusual place but when I was four years old I began to realise that the Works was a wonderful playground for my brother and me, see Fig. 10. but of course we did not always appreciate the dangers around us and my mother must have been desperately worried on occasions.

I think my father took the view that we had to take care of ourselves sometime but he also tried to check that the men looked after us as much as they were able. The Retort House was really the only place that was out of bounds to us but we seemed to get in there every now and then because it was so impressive.

Somehow or other I managed to fall into a large drum of green paint when I was about five and was covered in paint almost up to my shoulders. The canal, however, was the most dangerous area and my brother, before he learnt to swim, once fell in and was only saved from drowning because one of the men, Fred Whitehouse, happened to see him and pulled him out. In later years, I was told he was a very naughty boy.

One of his escapades involved a jar of strawberry jam. He took the jam from the pantry and wanted to find somewhere that he could eat it all without being seen. He decided that if he could climb up the vertical ladders and sit on top of one of the gasholders he would not be seen – remember he was only about 9 or 10 years old at the time. He didn't realise that a small boy with a jar of jam climbing to the top of a gasholder would in fact be very conspicuous. He was eventually rescued from the top and was severely reprimanded.

At that time in the early 1930's, the garden to our house was still very large and beautifully laid out stretching right down to the canal with an orchard, vegetable area and pig sties at the bottom. At the side of the garden was a field owned by the Company and beyond the hedge were another two fields which were bounded by the rear of the gardens to the houses in Alston Road, the canal and Wharf Lane. The last two fields were owned by Mr John Raven who lived at the Anchor Inn and he also owned some other fields by the Inn.

On the opposite side of the lane to our house and slightly further down was the Foreman's House which also had a large garden. For some years it had been occupied by Mr Kennard but when he retired in the early 1930's, Mr Fred Snow was appointed Foreman and lived

40

there with his wife, a daughter, Barbara and two sons, Phillip and Dennis.

Next down the lane after the Foreman's House were the two Stores mentioned earlier which at that time were in the charge of Fred Brown who had a moustache and always wore a flat cap. Behind was the Maintenance Shed occupied by Fred 'Ginty' Street, a bricklayer who did all the maintenance work with his labourer, Jack Warner, including repairs to the firebricks in the retorts – a very hot and unpleasant job.

I spent very many happy hours in that shed and around the Works with these two men during my school holidays. I must have been a blessed nuisance at the age of 5–11 years old but they were two very kind men and thoughtful workers who must have instilled in me an interest in all building work. One of my "jobs" was to help mix the red lead paint used in considerable quantities for priming on gasholders and other areas. I am sure the Health and Safety Executive would not approve of this activity now.

However, I enjoyed my "work" and training with the result that I learnt the rudimentary skills and tricks of the bricklayer and other skills which I still enjoy practising. Many years later, I decided I would like to become an architect, a decision not unconnected with the fun I had "helping" Ginty Street. During my working life as an Architect, many builders and tradesmen wondered why I knew so much about their work and dodges – it all began at a very early age.

At the end of the lane, just before the Anchor Inn, were various farm buildings used by Mr Raven for his cows and other animals and then of course there was the Inn of which he was the Publican. Prior to becoming landlord of the Anchor Inn, Mr Raven had been a gunsmith.

Besides being a great favourite with the gas workers, the Inn was now becoming very popular with the people from all the new houses that were being built in the Elmdon Heath area as it was the only inn close at hand at that time. It was to be some years before the Greville Arms was built at the end of Cornyx Lane in 1939 and the Anchor Inn closed.

Unfortunately, during the "Depression Years" of the early 1930's, there were a number of suicides when people threw themselves into the canal and drowned and I remember the ambulance coming down when they found a body. These incidents made quite a mark on me and once I thought I had seen a body and ran back to tell my mother

41

but fortunately it was only a waterlogged tree trunk.

The canal, the Grand Union, took a lot of barge traffic, some horse drawn and some with engines. During the winter it had to be kept clear of ice. It was a very impressive sight to see the ice breaker barge, which had a strengthened bow, coming along pulled by a team of horses charging down the tow path.

So far as I can recall, very little coal was delivered by barge by the early 1930's and certainly the main bulk of coal was brought by lorry from the railway sidings at Solihull Goods Yard. However, The Gas Company also paid Mr Raven, who employed a carter called Bill Corbett, to load coal from the Wharf and take it by horse and cart to the Retort House yard. Later on, Bill Corbett, with his clay pipe and twist of tobacco, was employed by the Company and he also helped bring coal by his horse and cart from the railway.

I am told that Bill Corbett, on his way back from the Goods Yard in Streetsbrook Road, would call in at the Barley Mow and pick up two quarts of beer which he then drank. The horse meanwhile would be slowly carrying on up Lode Lane and Bill would catch it up again after his drink.

One of my earliest memories was in fact of Bill Corbett and his horse and cart. They had just returned with a load of coal to the yard when the big carthorse called "Vic", trod on Bill's foot. It transpired later that Bill Corbett was well known for his colourful language and my brother and I must have heard his full range. We went straight back to our house and told our mother in great detail what had happened. I am sure that most of the words were new to her at that time and Bill was told by my father never to swear in front of us again – his foot must have been quite painful.

The horse and cart were gradually phased out as more lorries were used to transport all the coal from the railway. One of the early lorry drivers was Tom Pritchett, a kind and considerate man, who worked on the Gas Works for very many years and after retirement, he helped my mother and father in their garden. My wife and I used to visit Tom and his wife, in their retirement, and sampled Mrs Pritchett's barley wine at their house in Ulverley Green Road. Their grandson became one of the "Applejacks" group.

Another of the early drivers was Joe Beavan (see Fig. 11), who

Fig. 11 Gas fittings and meters were delivered in this early Ford van driven by Joe Beavan

was later to become a meter reader.

Because of the increase in transport by lorries, a new garage and workshop were built in 1935 just below the Foreman's house but are not shown on the aerial photograph. This garage housed the Morris Commercial lorry driven by Tom Pritchett and two Bedford 3–ton lorries which were to be purchased. One of the drivers of the new lorries was Joe Butler and the mechanic was his brother, George, who later worked for Rover at the Lode Lane works. Their other brother, Charlie, was one of the stokers in the Retort House.

There was always the odd bit of excitement on the Works, such as the time a fire broke out in the purifier beds when the lids were lifted off. The fire brigade was called but when the firemen turned their hoses on and poured water on the beds, the fumes given off caused the firemen to begin to pass out although the gas employees seemed unaffected – possibly they were used to it.

My brother and I were of course enthralled by the whole scene of flames and firemen collapsing on the ground. Somebody told us to run and get as much milk as possible from our house to help revive the casualties and this we did. I have since been told that milk was often thought to be good for gas poisoning but in fact this remedy was an "old wives' tale". True or false, the men recovered and the fire was put out.

By 1932, the number of houses in Solihull Urban District was increasing rapidly together with commercial premises and industry was also beginning to expand on new estates. The Gas Company had been preparing for this development because at the Annual General Meeting in the previous year, the Chairman, Mr Allday, stated that considerable sums of money had been spent on new mains, the Works had been highly re-modelled and gas production had increased threefold during the past ten years. A new coke screening plant had been installed which was a good investment and a Branch Showroom had been opened in Shirley.

The Chairman also said that the Company had always tried to satisfy demand and made the wise comment that, "expenditure was incurred but once but income continued in perpetuity". In the following year, Mr Allday had to retire as Chairman and Director due to ill health and Mr John Hall took over as Chairman.

I know we all tend to remember the good things of the past but everyone connected with Solihull Gas Company seemed to be part of a happy team. It was a tight knit community and all those whom I have met in later years said what a good spirit there had been and this extended through to the 1940 and 1950 decades. My father always involved himself in every detail of the operations as he had worked pushing hand carts and doing menial tasks on gas works when he served his apprenticeship and he understood the many problems that had to be faced.

I am told that in the '30s my father and mother took hot Christmas dinner to the men working in the old Retort House who were on the 6:00 a.m. to 2:00 p.m. shift and every year my father organised the Works Outing when he and all the men, see Figs. 12 and 13, went off together in a coach to various places such as Matlock although I doubt if many remembered much of the day if the number of beer crates I saw loaded aboard before they set off is anything to go by.

Jim Cliffe, who joined the Company as a gas fitter in 1938, tells me in that year he went on his first outing which was to Oxford where they went on the river. He had been advised beforehand not to

44

Fig. 12 & 13. Ready to leave on the "Works Outing"
– two have already developed a thirst at an early hour in the morning

join "the drinkers". He subsequently discovered this was good advice because the coach had not reached Warwick before the stone jars of beer were opened but there was never any trouble.

My father had arranged for a meal to be provided at Hampton-in-Arden on the way back. Jim had never seen so much food and none of them realised in two years time they would be in wartime and on rations.

There was also job security on the Works in those Depression Years of the late 20's and early 30's because the Gas Company after

Fig. 14. Some of the workers on the gas works – "a bunch of rogues"
Standing: Bill Corbett, Bill Green, Bill Beavan, Archie Smith, Fred
Devlin.
Sitting :   Fred Whitehouse, Ernie Coton, Frank Edgington, Charlie
Butler, George Butler, Arthur Mellings.

the Urban District Council was one of the biggest employers in the area with probably about 50 people.

Solihull Gas Company in 1930 was one of the first gas companies to allow Trade Union representation and employees were able to be members of the Transport and General Workers Union. Later on my father was instrumental in arranging a Pension Scheme for all the employees and some are still receiving pensions from this scheme. I believe this was the first such scheme in the country for gas workers.

I am not sure what hours were worked by the men but they all had to walk or ride a bicycle. Most lived in Elmdon Heath but one man, Tom Arnold, lived in a small cottage on the left hand side of the Warwick Road just past Haseley Five Ways on the way to Hatton. The cottage is still there and I often wonder how he managed to ride to work for 8.00 a.m. all through the winter and snow and no salting or road clearance in those days. He then did a hard days work after which he faced the return journey.

Some while ago I spoke to Ernie Marshall who originally worked on Knowle Gas Works but in 1934 he moved to Solihull Works as a driver bringing coal from the railway to Wharf Lane. He remembered most of the men shown on the photograph, Fig. 14., and smilingly described them as, "a bunch of rogues".

Other names are remembered by Mrs. Joan Pinfold, daughter of Fred Whitehouse and Mrs. Danton, daughter of Bill Corbett. Fred Whitehouse looked after the boilers on the works.

When each lorry arrived at the railway Goods Yard, the driver was directed to the waggons containing the coal for the Gas Works and he and his mate would then undo the doors in the side of the waggon and start to shovel out the coal into their lorry. They then drove to the Works and the coal was tipped into the coal yard. There was no mechanical handling.

Ernie recalled one particular day when the coal stocks at the Works were very low and he and his mate were asked to work overtime to overcome the problem. On that day, they shovelled 62 tons on to their lorry and delivered it to the Works which involved at least 20 trips – his was a 3 ton lorry. He said that they collapsed with exhaustion after the last load and couldn't do any more – no wonder!

Ernie Marshall, his mate and others are shown in Fig 15 and 16 in the midst of shovelling some of this coal. Ernie is the one with the trilby hat together with Oliver Jennings, his mate.

It will be appreciated that all this hard work for the lorry drivers and their mates and for the stokers in the Retort House raised a considerable thirst for all concerned. From my memory, and Ernie confirms it, the amount of ale drunk was very considerable and Ernie told me that there were some terrific "characters" on the Works and they were always playing practical jokes on each other but they were not malicious.

Figs. 15 & 16. A lot of coal had to be shovelled – all by hand

Earlier, I have mentioned Bill Corbett, and once again Ernie Marshall confirmed the stories about Bill who was a prodigious drinker, all from quart bottles. Frank "Grippem" Edgington, it appears followed him as a close second.

Jim Cliffe, has told me about an incident in later years during wartime when he, Frank Edgington and some other men were in the Mess Room and Frank had severe toothache. It was suggested that the best answer was to remove the offending tooth and, with Frank's agreement, one man tied one end of some strong string round the tooth and the other end round the door knob with the door open. When Frank Edgington was steadied on his feet, another man slammed the door shut and Jim Cliffe was astounded by this crude but efficient method of extraction. The tooth shot out together with part of the gum and a fair amount of blood.

However, Frank quickly recovered himself and stated that, "there was nothing a couple of quarts of beer would not put right", and promptly walked out to take this self-prescribed medicine. There is no record as to any lasting damage that Frank may have suffered.

One other important person on the Works was Len Allen, the Mains Superintendent, another delightful man who ensured that all the gas mains were in order and was also involved in all the new mains which were being laid for new and future developments. Len Allen was also a water diviner and would often use his skill to check on any water problems that there might be before they excavated any trenches.

I spent many happy hours travelling round the district in his van viewing all the work that was going on and to this day I have considerable interest in digging trenches and excavations. The amount of work to be overseen by Len Allen was considerable because not only was he involved with new mains, but also with alterations to existing mains and connections to all the new customers. It was reported that a large amount of money was spent on new mains and there was a big increase in customers in 1930 and 1931 but the figures through the 1930's show the full extent of the expansion.

49

	New mains laid	New Customers
1932	*Not known*	350
1933	6 miles	631
1934	9 1/2 miles	600
1935	8 miles	858
1936	14 1/2 miles	845
1937	12 1/2 miles	(
1938	*Not known*	(1318 (
	76 miles (Known total)	4602 (Known total)

The total of all previous and new customers by 1938 was 9,038 and rising fast. These figures reflect the rapid development of Solihull during this time and the amount of coal brought from the Railway Station, all of which still had to be shovelled by hand, was as follows:

1885	660 Tons
1931	6,053 Tons
1938	16,117 Tons

However it was not all hard work and leisure times were enjoyed to the full. I have mentioned the field owned by John Raven behind the houses in Alston Road and it was the highlight of our year when the circus came and was held in this field. We would be awake at first light, looking out of our bedroom window and waiting for the first vehicles to come round the corner from Cornyx Lane and drive down Wharf Lane. Many of the large trailers were pulled by steam traction engines or lorries so you can imagine it was an impressive sight.

They all turned into the field through the gateway by the side of the large oak tree just in front of our house. We would then go down to "help" put up the Big Top but most important of all we would show them to the very large water tank which was at the bottom of our garden. As this was the nearest water supply available, all the animals, other than those which were too dangerous, were brought to the tank to be watered. The most exciting were the elephants who lumbered down the field but one day, a kangaroo, who had been brought by his keeper, escaped and started jumping all round the field and it was a while before he was caught – we all enjoyed that and we also got free tickets to the Circus in exchange for the drinking arrangements for the animals.

One year the Circus was held in one of Mr Raven's other fields behind the Anchor Inn alongside the canal. That was "Lord Sangers" Circus and it was opened by Claud Dampier, the comedian.

Another very important annual event in pre-war Solihull was Carnival Day and one year somebody suggested that it would be a good idea to have hot dog stalls on the route but how could they do the cooking? My father, who was on the Carnival Committee, said they could leave it to him.

On Carnival Day, early in the morning, a gas workman went to each of the three chosen positions on the route, one in Cornyx Lane, one in the High Street and a third in Park Road at the entrance to Malvern Park. The pavements were dug up at each site adjoining a suitable lamp post, the gas main in the pavement was exposed and a connection made to the gas pipe. A second hand gas cooker was then placed on the pavement in each position and a gas fitter came along to connect up each of the cookers. All was then ready for the lady Carnival helpers in the afternoon to come along and start cooking – no problem.

At the end of the day, the cookers were disconnected, the pavements made good and the connections were left for the following year – they may still be there! Today, that sort of action would require all emergency services standing by and the road closed following an Act of Parliament which would have been required in the first place. Things were far more straightforward in those days.

Another source of entertainment occurred in 1938 and 1939 when Silhillians had the chance to see aircraft at close quarters when Sir

Alan Cobham brought his air display to Solihull and occupied the big field bounded by Widney Manor Road, Browns Lane and Smiths Lane. Quite a number of aeroplanes took part and when I now look at the field I wonder how the aircraft took off in this restricted area, but they did. I know the trees have grown since that time but even so they restricted the take off to some extent, and with all the cars and spectators down the side of the field, it was very exciting.

It was at the first display in 1938 that my father booked three seats for a flight suitably described as, "A Trip round the Gas Works". I think our 'plane was called an Airspeed Ferry which held about six and up I went with my father and brother and around the Works as promised. The aerial photograph of the Works was taken earlier in about 1934–35, unconnected with the air display, but it provides a valuable slice of Solihull history.

On the corner of Cornyx Lane and Wharf Lane was a shop and post office (the shop is still there but it has been extended) for General Stores and Groceries run by Mr and Mrs Barnes. Mr. Barnes had been a Sergeant Major in the Regular Army as a musketry instructor and still had his waxed moustache. He later became Sergeant Major

Fig. 17. In 1936 the author was still able to ride a horse
in the adjoining field which in 1938 was to be used for a new
Retort House, coal yard and offices.

52

to the O.T.C. for a number of years at Solihull School.

Mr and Mrs Barnes were a very pleasant couple and had two children, Fred, who later became a very keen trials motor cyclist and ran a cycle shop on the Warwick Road opposite to Mill Lane, and Joan, who was the first girl at Malvern Hall to win a Major Open Scholarship in 1939/40 – to Newnham College, Cambridge. The shop was a great asset to the area and we were regular customers.

My mother and father always used to go to Braggs, the butchers, in Station Road opposite Poplar Road and now the site of Barclays Bank. Alfred Bragg and his two sons, Horace and Norman, ran the shop and their meat was delivered in an extremely smartly turned out horse and yellow painted trap. Mr Alfred Bragg sold my father two or three horses over the years for our use although one had to go back because he kept throwing us off.

Up to 1936, we had the use of the field at the side of our garden so my brother and I were able to ride our horse in this field, see Fig. 17, and the horse was kept in a stable at the bottom of the garden. Hay was available from Mr Raven who harvested the two adjoining fields. Mr Raven did not have a tractor so horses pulled the mower to cut the hay beginning round the edge of the fields. As the amount of hay got smaller in the middle of the fields, the men got out their guns ready to shoot the rabbits which came out of the hay as the mower got close. The hay was then gathered in with the horse drawn hay rake and a haystack was built at the side of the field.

Our horses and many of the other horses in the district went to the blacksmith in Damson Lane, almost opposite the end of Alston Road, for shoeing. The blacksmith was called Jim Cotton and he worked there from 1924 to 1949. He also did a lot of work for the Gas Company repairing and sharpening tools and he even did work for the Knowle Gas Company.

The gas works at Knowle must have been a very similar age to those at Solihull but obviously smaller and some time, I am not sure when, in the early 1930's Solihull Gas Company took over Knowle Gas Company. The Works in Station Road, Dorridge, carried on for a while until it closed in 1937 after which all gas to that area was supplied from the Solihull Works.

All old Silhillians will remember going to the gas showroom in

Mill Lane to choose their gas fire or cooker and to pay their bills. With the housing boom, many more appliances were being sold, so many that in 1932, the Showroom was extended at the back to double the sales area.

In charge of the Showroom was Mrs Biddle, who with her assistants one of whom was called Joan Catton, dealt with the extra demand for all types of gas appliances. The sales of gas cookers and fires had steadily been rising and marketing of the new "Ascot" water heaters had just begun helped on by their representative, Mr Walter Hoe, who lived in Lode Lane opposite the old Workhouse. Appliance sales in 1933 were a record, followed by a large increase in 1934 and another record of 1,240 sales in 1935. A new product in 1935 was the gas refrigerator which also helped boost sales.

The number of office staff was also growing. There was an Accounts Office on the ground floor and the whole of the first floor was now used for offices. When Mrs Ainsworth and her family vacated the top floor in the early 30's, this area also became offices.

A full description of the offices and its occupants during the War years is given in the next chapter by Miss Vere Smith who was one of the staff at that time.

The driveway at the right hand side of the Showroom led to the Yard behind in which there were the Stores for cookers, fires, gas pipes, fittings and meters. There were also other outbuildings on the left for the meter readers and fitters.

The main Store was looked after by a rather severe looking man with white hair called Mr Bennett, who always seemed to wear a black suit, and who lived in Lode Lane at the junction with Moat Lane. He was an excellent organiser and a strict disciplinarian who would inspect the fitters' tools at regular intervals to see if they needed replacing. If he saw a screwdriver with a damaged end – he would say, "that's what happens when you use a hammer on it, you don't deserve another – keep it". Behind the counter in the Store was Andy Logan.

It was because of Andy Logan that I learnt the meaning of the word, "accent". I had great difficulty in understanding what Andy Logan said and up to that time I thought everybody spoke in the same way. It was explained to me that Andy came from Scotland and people from there speak in a different way, just the same as people in other parts of England in other words they speak with a different accent. I appreciated this explanation but I still could not understand what Andy said – his was a very "broad accent"!

Other names I recall among the meter readers and fitters are Lew Ashley, Dumigam, Ward, Berry, Tom Coleman, Walter Lawrence, Jim Cliffe, Jerry Glissett, and Joe Beavan. Joe Beavan was a loyal worker for Solihull Gas Company from the time he joined the Company when he left the Army after the 1914–18 War. He had done various jobs on the Works prior to taking on a position as meter reader and this job he did for many years until his retirement in 1958. In his spare time, Joe Beavan had helped my father in the garden at our house in Marsh Lane for many years. Even after his retirement and that of my father, he still visited my father and did odd jobs. I am sure there was a strong bond between them and they enjoyed reminiscing about old times – the odd jobs were not quite as important.

I understand from his son, Stanley, that the last entry in his father's diary was a visit to my father the day before Joe Beavan died. Incidentally, Stanley Beavan has written an excellent book on the local history of Elmdon Heath called, "Damson by the Pound", which includes some graphic accounts of the Gas Works.

Above the main Stores, was the Sports Club run for the use of all employees and it was in this area that many children had been taught to cook in the 1920's. There was a snooker table, darts and card tables and concerts were also held in this room. The concerts were rather riotous affairs but everyone had a good time and so helped the team spirit in the Company.

The meter readers and gas fitters had to get round the whole Solihull Urban District on their bicycles which were very heavy machines with a large carrier on the front to hold their weighty tools and money from the slot meters. It has to be remembered that by the late 1930's and early 1940's gas was supplied not only to Solihull, Knowle, Shirley and Earlswood but also to Hampton-in-Arden.

The meter readers, See Fig, 18, in their heavy uniforms and caps, besides reading the quarterly meters, had to empty out the slot or coin meters and the weight of the coins at the end of the day was

Fig. 18. Meter Readers at Mill Lane
Joe Beavan, Eric Pyke, Archie Maynard, Ernest Berry, Cyril Ward

heavy so the men had to be very fit to ride their bicycles over these long distances in all sorts of weather. They then took their heavy leather bags full of money into the Accounts Office in Mill Lane to be counted.

New cookers, fires, meters, pipes and fittings were distributed round the district by van driven by Bill Smitten but most of the meter readers plodded round on their bikes until the very end of Solihull Gas Company in about 1962.

Another familiar sight round Solihull District was the lamp-lighter. Until the 1940's practically all street lighting in Solihull was by gas and these lamps had to be lit and the mantles, the equivalent to light bulbs, had to be changed. The lamp-lighters, who were usually employed by the Council, rode around on their bicycles with their tools in a bag and a short ladder over their shoulder so that they could climb up the lamp-posts.

In the early days of street lighting in Solihull, each gas light, and there were about 100 in 1904 and increasing all the time, had to be lit individually every night and switched off the next morning. The lamp-lighter used a long wooden pole to operate the gas tap in the light and the gas in the mantle ignited to give a bright whitelight.

All gas lights, whether they were street lights or lights in the home, had gas mantles which were about the size of an egg cup and were made of a white gauze impregnated with certain types of oxides. The gauze formed the outside of the mantle just the same as glass in a light bulb. When gas was let into the mantle, it would then be lit and air would be drawn in through the gauze which resulted in an intense white light being given off from the mantle.

Later on each street lamp was fitted with a clockwork time clock which turned on and switched off the gas tap on the light at the appropriate time. The lamp-lighter still had to change the times on the clocks at set intervals and to change the mantles when needed.

Transport was provided for these men in later years but there was at least one lamp-lighter in Solihull with his bike and ladder still very active until all gas lighting gave way to electricity, probably in the 1950's.

The Directors of the Gas Works had come to the conclusion in 1935 that new plant would have to be provided to deal with the ever rising demand for gas which had reached 186 million cubic feet in that year. At that time, the Chairman was Mr Robert Bragg J.P. of Bragg Bros., Builders, in Church Hill Road (opposite Witley Avenue), the best known and very reputable builders in Solihull at that time.

Mr Bragg had been appointed Chairman in 1934 when Mr Hall retired due to ill health and it was he who was to be the leader of the biggest expansion due to take place over the next few years. For the record, Mr E P Currall and Mr P W Allday had been appointed Directors in 1933 and my father was to be elected later as a Director, General Manager and Secretary.

A decision was made to use the most up-to-date equipment and to build a new vertical Retort House, a new purifier plant, condenser, a 10,000,000 cubic feet gasholder and a carburetted water gas plant – the cost totalling £50,301.

Contracts were signed in 1936 and work began. The only problem for my family was that the only room for expansion was in our garden,

Fig. 19. Our garden began to reduce in size

see Fig. 19. and the adjoining field where my horse was kept. By March 1937, we had lost over half our garden and all the field.

A new fully mechanised purifier plant had been built, see Figs. 19 & 20. in our garden which rather overshadowed us. A very tall water tower had been built behind and Woodhall Duckam had built the vertical Retort House in the field together with new Works offices and weighbridge, a new roadway and coal and coke yard areas. The Retort House was quite an impressive building, about 100 feet high, with large white letters across the front reading "USE GAS". See Fig. 21.

It was intended that coal should again be brought to the Works by canal and a new wharf built. The coal was to be loaded from the barges and taken to the top of the Retort House by bucket elevator. Unfortunately, it seems that this method of feeding coal at high level by elevator was not a success as when the plant came into operation for the first time, the whole building filled with coal dust as the coal dropped on the conveyor belt feeding the hoppers and all the stokers rushed out of the building to escape the dust and breathe again.

Fig. 20. The new purifier plant built in the garden

Fig. 21. The vertical Retort House built in 1937 advertised,"USE GAS"; a repeat installation was added to the left of the original in 1941

59

Presumably the problem was not solved to everyone's satisfaction because very soon coal was again being brought by road from the railway and loaded into the retort in some other way.

Except for this one hiccup, the new plant was far more efficient with the vertical retorts being able to be fully loaded compared with the old horizontal retorts where space had to be left round the coal. The new retorts also meant that the loading and unloading were done by gravity so the physical work was considerably reduced. The handling of the coal and coke was also far more mechanised.

The proximity of the canal to the Retort House is shown in Fig. 22, the elevator that was going to bring the coal up from the barges having been long removed.

A considerable amount of coke was now being produced but fortunately the demand for this smokeless fuel had increased with well designed small and large boilers on the market. Coke was fed

Fig. 22. The Retort House had been built close to the canal so that coal could be delivered by barge

60

into lorries from overhead hoppers and the whole coke distribution and sorting plant was very much larger and more mechanised than the old one. However, one aspect of the old plant remained, "Oily Bill" Whitehouse had just moved across the Works to the new plant and soon imposed his usual control over operations.

People also came to collect coke for use in their homes and later on, when fuel was short, customers would come from far and wide with all sorts of transport including wheelbarrows and some even brought prams to be filled up.

In 1936/37 there was a very severe winter. The new plant had been completed just in time as there was an exceptional demand which showed that even more high and low pressure mains were needed.

The carburetted water gas plant, which had also been built, was used to supplement the coal gas from the Retort House. The plant, built by Humphreys and Glasgow, produced "water gas" which had the advantage that it could be brought into action quickly. If there was a sudden demand, it was then mixed with the coal gas. However, the "water gas" had less calorific value so could only be used in a proportion usually not exceeding 25% otherwise the resultant mixture of gas would be diluted too much. The Water Gas plant was built just behind the old Boiler House next to the canal.

The whole of the field was now being developed because a new road was laid from Wharf Lane down the line of the boundary hedge to the new Retort House and Coal Yard. Half way down the road, a small Works Office block and weighbridge were built. All lorries carrying coal and coke now entered and left the Works by this road so that their weights could be checked.

Some of the work was carried out by the Works' own employees, in addition to their ordinary jobs, and Ernie Marshall remembered being in charge of removing the hedges and helping excavate for the new road and yard areas.

The new offices included the weighbridge office staffed by Don Galloway and a young clerk called Jackson, both of whom were to go in the Army during the War. The other ground floor office was occupied by Mr Pinder who was the Works Manager at that time and one of the first floor offices became the Chemist's Laboratory. All these developments meant that the Gas Works would now have considerable capacity but it is interesting to note that the price of gas had been held for many years and was a very economical fuel.

The last big addition to the Works was a fourth gasholder, far bigger than the three existing holders, and this was built on spare land just past the previous largest holder and before the Anchor Inn. This holder was a spirally guided type and before it was commissioned, I had the thrill of going inside the holder – it was rather like a huge cave.

Whilst the holder was being built, one of the steel erectors brought his son, aged about 14, to the Works one Sunday morning and took him to the top, about 100 feet high, so that he could get used to heights and follow in his father's footsteps. The opposite happened – the poor boy was terrified and was in a very pitiful state when they walked back up the lane. I often wondered what happened to him and what line of work he took up in later years.

Whilst all this expansion took place, war clouds were looming and just before the war, in 1938–39, air raid precautions were taking place. Air raid shelters were being created by the men digging trenches at the side of the new road and these were then covered over with the timber grids taken from the old purifier beds and then a good thickness of earth and turf was placed on top.

A Donkins of Chesterfield fire pump with hoses and trailer was obtained and this was towed by one of the lorries with George Butler in charge. I remember one practice run that took place with a fire being lit on the open land, now Heath Gardens, behind Cornyx Lane and the lorry being driven as fast as possible from the Works to the fire – all very exciting. A barrage balloon was later positioned on this site and I recall, in September 1939 as war was declared, seeing this barrage balloon going up for the first time.

Quickly returning to 1930, my brother had been going to a small school in George Road but, when Eversfield School opened on the Warwick Road in 1931, he and then I in 1932, used to walk to this school up Hermitage Road, over Lode Lane, and then across a field to the end of Manor Road which at that time stopped at the junction with Thornby Avenue.

In 1938, Manor Road was extended a small way towards Lode Lane and a few more houses built on either side but there was still open land and a footpath from Lode Lane to the end of Manor Road.

In 1939, the Headmaster at Eversfield School, Mr Denney, decided that in the event of war, if the air raid warning sounded, all those boys who could get back home in five minutes need not stay in the cellars at the school. All those boys who thought they could get home within five minutes, rode as fast as they could on their bicycles. I was one of them and I was very relieved that I managed to get home within the time limit. Presumably all the parents had to report back to Mr Denney on the result of the exercise.

In my innocence, I did not realise that the Gas Works would be a prime target but when you are young, it is always better to be at home in times of trouble.

We had all been issued with gas masks in cardboard boxes and one day all the boys from Eversfield School were walked in classes to "The Grove" in Lode Lane where a gas chamber had been built. We had to put on our gas masks and go into this chamber in groups. The room was then filled with gas of some sort and this was supposed to check that we knew how to wear masks and that they worked – they did.

At that time, it was also reported in the local newspaper that Solihull Gas Company was leading the way in air raid precautions and 26 employees had passed an anti-poison gas course – I wonder if it was the one that we did.

Unbeknown to me in 1938, when we had lost almost all our garden and we were surrounded by the new installations, my father decided that we would have to move and he had plans prepared for a new house which was to be built in Marsh Lane, Solihull.

Our house had remained exactly the same as it was when built in about 1912–14, the same old sinks, bathroom, and of course, no electricity; in fact so far as I recall, there was no electricity on the Works, other than for pumps etc., until 1937 and then only in the new Retort House. The new offices built at the same time had gas lighting installed, after all it would have been very bad advertisement to have electric lighting on a Gas Works!

My father always said that gas lights, "were easier on the eyes" and people would not have to wear glasses so long as they stuck to gas lighting – "you do not get flickering like electric light bulbs".

Unlike most people at that time, we changed gas mantles, not electric bulbs, and we were used to the faint hiss of the gas and pulling the chains up and down from the lights to turn them on and off.

It was, therefore, in the summer of 1939 that all was to change and we moved into our new house in Marsh Lane – with electricity, but just in case, my father had gas lights installed, one in each room for emergency purposes; after all, electricity could sometimes fail which of course it did on occasions during the War so we then returned to gas. We had gas fires in every room and we also had a gas refrigerator and gas water heaters over the sink and one basin in case of emergency!

It was also in 1939 that Mr Pinder retired and Mr Stephen Downes became the new Works Manager and he and his wife moved into our old house. I am sure some improvements must have been made.

During 1939, the Company was still expanding and I have no doubt that there were many meetings with various bodies concerning problems if war broke out, which by that time was almost certain. "Shadow Factories" had been planned and built to replace factories which could be destroyed in wartime and the largest was in Lode Lane on the opposite side of the canal to the Works, which subsequently became the "Rover Works".

All these factories would require gas and provision would also have been required for making good damage to gas mains, other installations and of course the Gas Works itself.

During the year, six extra miles of gas mains had been laid, there had been 535 new customers and £1,364 had been spent on Civil Defence Work – all reported at the Annual General Meeting. It was also said that a new boiler house with two boilers had been built together with a duplicate water gas plant and a high pressure gas receiver and so Solihull Gas Company continued its expansion at a considerable rate. But war broke out in September 1939 and different problems would then have to be faced.

Chapter 7

Through wartime, nationalisation and the closure of the Works, 1939–1962

My first memory after the Prime Minister, Neville Chamberlain, announced that this country was at war with Germany on 3rd September 1939, was going up to my bedroom, looking out of the window and seeing the barrage balloon being raised into the air from its site behind Cornyx Lane in Elmdon Heath. I suppose the first impact on the Gas Works was that no gas would be required at night for all the street lamps as the "Black Out" began straightaway and the lamps would not be lit again for another six years.

From the personal aspect, quite a number of the men were to be called up into the Services during the ensuing years but I think the first man to have left was Army Reservist, Ernie Marshall. He had received his recall papers and for him the War was to be a very unpleasant experience. First of all he was sent to France and then had to escape in the evacuation but eventually he was sent out to Singapore just as Japan entered the War and invaded Malaya. It appears that his regiment landed but all their guns had not been shipped with them. They had to find any guns that were available and then start to fight.

With the collapse of Singapore, Ernie was taken prisoner and was in Japanese prisoner of war camps before finally being taken to Japan where he was lucky to survive having lost many of his comrades on the voyage.

Jim Bastock who was in the T.A. was called up immediately and so was Fred Whitehouse who was a Reservist having previously been in the Regular Army. Fred was sent to France and was lucky to escape at Dunkirk. Bill Smitten and Bill Conway were also called up but I have no information about all the other men who were called up nor if they all survived.

So far as my father was concerned, his duty in the event of air raids, was to report to the Police Station in Poplar Road. Throughout the War, the telephone in our house would ring, first of all the caller would say that there was a "Yellow Warning" which meant an air raid was likely, then there was another call to give a "Purple Warning" – air raid imminent – whereupon my father would get up and drive to the Police Station. At this time, air raids were usually at night and when the third telephone call came through giving a "Red Warning", you could already hear the bombers overhead and the anti-aircraft fire.

There were many false alarms early in the War and it was not until the summer of 1940 that there were air raid warnings almost every night and so he was out all the time until the "All Clear" sounded. As bombs began to fall in the Solihull Urban District, my father had to be available to go to any incident where damage may have occurred to gas mains and emergency repairs were required or the gas closed off. This was quite dangerous work and was also extra responsibility for Len Allen, the Mains Superintendent and all concerned had many busy nights. I still have my father's map of the District with all the gas mains marked on and the emergency telephone numbers.

One early morning on his return, my father told us that three bombs had landed on the High Street so I decided to take a look on my way to school and saw that the "White Cat" (now called The Fat Cat) had been hit. "Fitters" clock shop had been destroyed with bits of watches and clocks all over the street and the front of "Winfields" chemist shop was blown in. Don Galloway and his clerk, (was it Peter?) Jackson, were called up and I believe it was then that Frank Weston, who was crippled with arthritis, and Frank Turner took over the running of the Works Office and weighbridge.

Other men were called up and older men were brought in to replace them. In mid-1940 there were only four fitters left at Mill Lane but in any case there was very little work for them to do. No gas appliances such as cookers and fires were available and materials were in very short supply except for emergency use.

Jim Cliffe, one of the fitters, was sent to the Works to carry out some pipework but, when he had finished, he was rather dismayed to be told by the Foreman, Fred Snow, that the situation was very serious and he would be staying. Fred told him that there would be no more shopping with Mrs. Cliffe on Saturday afternoons, there would be no time to go to church on Sundays, and if Jim had any spare time after that, the Company would use that as well!

Every man had to be prepared to do any job and to work all hours. The fitters and meter readers were also called in to help in the worst job of all, cleaning out the purifier beds. Fred Brown, the storeman, gave them all "pecks" and shovels and they were told to get on with it. Even those who were not able-bodied had to help in cleaning up and the men were not allowed to walk into their houses when they had finished because they smelt so much from the iron oxide they had been handling.

Later on in 1942 my father even obtained the release for 6 months of Fred Whitehouse who had suffered at Dunkirk and later on he was released again so desperate was the labour position.

Another man who came to the Works was Dom O'Donnell and this came about because one day in 1940, he met Len Allen in the Red Lion who told him that they urgently needed help on the Gas Works. Dom had been a builder before the War and had been constructing air raid shelters but these had all been completed so he accepted the offer and started work as a driver.

He told me that other lorries were then being driven by Bert Strangewood with his mate, Mick Mathews, and Mick Marshall with his mate, "Little Johnny". Other drivers were Tom Sutheran and Harry Evetts – Harry had previously been a driver at Knowle Gas Works and still wore breeches and leggings from his horse and cart days.

The normal daily target for Dom O'Donnell was to unload 20 tons of coal from the railway waggons at the Goods Station and take it to the Works in his 2–ton hopper lorry. This meant ten journeys and all loading was still done by hand. Dom also helped load coke into the Water Gas Plant.

Replacement labour was also provided by five or six women who were drafted in to do war work. The work was very hard for these women, one of whom was called Nance Green and another Ida Bayliss, as they were employed as labourers bagging up coke and other jobs. Dom O'Donnell remembered taking them up the "Village" during their lunch break to do their shopping and then taking them back to work. I am not sure if the lorry was empty or full of coal.

It was towards the end of 1940 that the Company decided that further expansion of the Works would have to take place as the adjoining Shadow Factory was then in full production towards the war effort and they needed all the gas they could get. Other firms were gradually moving out from Birmingham, particularly when the air raids began, so it was agreed that capacity would have to be increased and the Retort House extended.

Dom O'Donnell, being a builder, was given the task of digging out the foundations ready for Woodhall Duckham to build a repeat of the Retort House which they had built in 1937. He was helped by a strange team of men consisting of a Swedish Sea Captain, who still wore his Captain's hat while digging, his Ship's Engineer and two Norwegian sailors. Apparently the four men had been stranded in this country early in the War and had obviously been offered work, though goodness knows how they arrived in Solihull.

It seems that a considerable amount of earth had to be moved particularly because the top four feet was spoil on top of the original ground at the time when the canal was formed. The five men then had to dig further down until a firm footing had been reached – no mean task. However, as soon as the excavations had been completed, Woodhall Duckham began construction and the new Retort House was quickly built and in production later in 1941. Dom stayed to help until it was finished and then returned to his driving and more shovelling!

The original Retort House with "USE GAS", with the second repeat Retort House built alongside, can be seen on Fig. 21. The big lettering was however not repeated; the Works was already a big enough target for bombers without further advertisement, although all the buildings had been painted in camouflage colours.

Twice as much coal was now needed and one day the coal supplies almost ran out. Luckily, somebody, probably Fred Snow who was

68

still the Works Foreman, remembered some "German Reparation Coal" delivered to the Works after the end of the 1914–18 War – over 20 years ago. Grass had grown over it and the men had to clear the grass and earth away before they could dig the coal out and place it in the hopper in the new Retort House. From the hopper, the coal went into the "kibbler" or "crusher" but unfortunately Dom O'Donnell did not know that the new kibbler was different from the old one and the coal was not suitable for it. They then had to set to getting it all out again before placing it in the right hopper. It is not recorded what was said at the time.

I understand that at the time, because of the demand for gas by factories, my father told the Ministry of Fuel and Power that he would shut the Works down if he did not get more coal supplies. This had the desired effect and the problem was never repeated.

One day a whole trainload of coal arrived at Solihull Station and every vehicle available was pressed into service. Jim Cliffe remembers all sorts of lorries, even Council dust carts, arriving and there was coal everywhere.

A very sad event happened in daylight early one morning when a lone bomber flew very low over Solihull. I saw this aircraft from my bedroom window as it circled round over Berry Hall and Hampton Lane towards Elmdon Heath. The bomber continued to turn and flew in at a very low level towards the Gas Works. The men on the Works said they saw the bombs begin to drop but because the aircraft was so low, the bombs bounced off the ground and landed on houses in Alston Road and Cornyx Lane. I never knew if this version was true but unfortunately a whole family were killed in one of the houses in Cornyx Lane and there were others injured in nearby houses.

However, when I was speaking to Dom O'Donnell, he confirmed to me that the story was true and described to me the furrows in the ground where the bombs bounced. Jim Cliffe also remembers the incident and how one of the bomb's fins was ripped off when it hit the ground.

The air raid warning had been given and he and Bill Corbett were in the Mess Room at the time. Bill, who never drank any other liquid except beer, had just reached for two quart bottles from under the sink when the bombs exploded. It seems that Bill was very badly

69

shocked by the tragedy as his own family lived in Alston Road and they knew the family who had been killed. Bill finished work soon afterwards and it was not long before he died in retirement.

The next day, German radio announced that a gas works to the east of Birmingham had been destroyed. A lucky escape for the gas works and the men on it but a tragedy for those who had been killed and injured in nearby houses.

Fuel was obviously in short supply during the war years and there was one advertisement in the local paper headed – "Appeal to save fuel"

"If everyone of us took one cup of tea less every day, it would save enough gas in a month to make 69,200 bombs"

I believe that this notice was issued by the Ministry of Fuel and Power or the Ministry of Information to all gas companies for them to publish. There must have been very little gas used in making each bomb! Facts have a habit of being overlooked in wartime.

One grain of comfort for the men who were working all hours was that the Ministry of Food granted them extra rations. Each man was allowed 1 oz. of tea, 2 oz. butter and 4 oz. of sugar every four weeks and if Moyle and Adams, the grocers in High Street, had any extra biscuits they had those as well!

Dom O'Donnell also told me a little story concerning one customer who presumably had a little difficulty in obtaining fuel:

"Bill Weston in the Works Office asked me, as he frequently did, to deliver a load of coke to a customer on my way home. Previously I had delivered to such as Forward Engineering, W G Gameson and Woolmans and I would be able to have the cost of the transport – a nice drop of beer for me!

This customer, Arthur Coton was his name, came out of his house and said – 'tip it there' – I said I was a transport contractor for "The Gas" and just wanted the same figure for delivering it as "The Gas" would have charged, namely 18/- (old money). He came close to me and said – 'do you realise I have been a customer for over 40 years? – I'll get to the bottom of this!'

He went back to his house and 'phoned "The Gas". Bill Weston must have given him a mouthful – he came running down the alley with a pound note in his hand – 'Keep the change', he said. We had a good laugh the following morning – Bill giving us one of his big smiles. God bless him – always cheerful in spite of his pain."

Dom O'Donnell carried on working as a driver until the end of the War in 1945.

It was sometime during the War that my father took me with him to see the Gas Works at Henley-in-Arden. I would think it was perhaps one of the smallest Works in the country. The Works was built in 1862 for a cost of £1,600. It was a private company which was formed to provide gas to Henley-in-Arden – the builder was the principal shareholder.

The Works was built on a site at the far end of Beaudesert Lane on the right hand side and really was miniature in size. Pre-war, it had been run by two men but during the War, Jim Horseley with the help of his wife, ran the Works on his own. The Retort House was extremely small and there was one very little gasholder. It was an almost impossible task for Jim Horseley to operate the Works on his own which he had to do, 24 hours a day and every day of the year. As a result, Mr and Mrs Horseley never had a holiday and goodness knows what happened if Jim Horseley was ill – perhaps he was not allowed to be, but on many occasions gas pressure in Henley-in-Arden was very poor.

I was assured that it was a true story that there were instances at Sunday lunchtime when demand was greatest, Mr and Mrs Horseley had to eat their dinner sitting on the gasholder to create extra pressure. Whether this story was true or not, Solihull Gas Company was called in to see if they could help and in fact they took over the running of the Works much to the relief of the two Directors, Mr Norman Welch and Mr F.S. Lodder, and certainly to Jim Horseley.

In due course, I understand that a new main was laid to Henley-in-Arden and after that the residents of Henley had a constant supply of gas. I am not sure when Henley Gas Works actually closed, possibly in the early 1950's because in 1948, at the request of the Ministry of

Fuel and Power prior to nationalisation, Solihull Gas Company were requested to acquire the majority of the shares of Henley-in-Arden Gas, Coal and Coke Co Ltd and this they did.

In due course, the Works was demolished and a number of houses were built on the site but prior to that it was reported that during the short time that Solihull Gas Company had looked after the Henley Works, the situation had much improved with great benefit to the consumers in the Henley area.

Back in Solihull, still during wartime, little had altered at the Gas Showroom and Offices in Mill Lane. I often called in to see my father in his office and in particular used to see his Secretary, Miss Lane, who lived in Station Road, Knowle and the Chief Clerk, Mr Horace Clewer who lived in St Helens Road. However, I have received a letter from Miss Vere E Smith who worked in the Accounts Department, which describes the offices, Showroom and all the people who worked there at that time. Here is the letter with thanks to Miss Smith:

SOLIHULL GAS COMPANY, Mill Lane, Solihull

I worked at the Mill Lane Offices of the Solihull Gas Company just prior to and during the War. Mill Lane ran from the High Street to Warwick Road, and the Gas Offices were located about 200 yards down the street on the left-hand side. On the other side of the road were friendly terraced cottages with pocket handkerchief front gardens. The Gas Office building was originally, I believe, a house or two large houses, converted into one large building. First, were the offices and a front door opening into a passage and leading to all the offices. (This was the staff entrance). The other half of the building on the ground floor was the large showroom with plate glass display window. Three members of staff were kept busy on duty there. (I remember a Mrs Biddle, Manageress, and a Miss Catton). At the side of the showroom, running from the front to the back of the area, was the Gas Yard. There were out-houses adjoining the main building and this was where all repairs and maintenance jobs were done. The Supervisor was a silver haired Mr Bennet.

The Manager and Company Secretary, Mr S.J. Sadler, occupied the front office on the first floor, as did his Chief Clerk, Mr Clewer in an office on that floor, and the Knowle Office Clerk, Miss Lane. The telephone room was also on that floor, and on the floor above was the Staff Rest Room.

I was employed in the Accounts Dept., (front Office ground floor) and three of us took care of the books plus our Junior whom we christened "Bimbo". Our desk was one long, large, sloping wooden one at which my colleague and I sat. Our supervisor was a Mrs Chambers, and she sat at a table and dealt with all queries on accounts. Our ledgers were about 24" x 24" and bound and we sat on high stools to post the Shirley and Solihull Quarterly Accounts. My colleague was a Miss Wheeldon – she had a lovely soprano voice, and later left the office to join the WAAF – singing with their concert party, and later after the War, with the Sadlers Wells Company. The meter men wore navy blue uniforms – each rode a bike, and came into the office every afternoon to bring either their quarterly or slot meter book, from the area in which they had been working. This time was always interesting as there would be a feedback about customers and events in certain areas and any problems arising. (I remember a Mr Berry and a Mr Tustin).

We were a friendly family of employees and co-operation was the key from the Manager through the whole staff. (Quite secretly, I think our Manager SJS as we called him, had trained as a sportsman, as he always seemed to mount and descend the stairs at great speed).

On the corner of Mill Lane and the High Street was Davis's the Bakery, and the aroma of baking bread on certain days spurred everyone's appetite.

Rima's Cafe was situated at the Warwick Road end of Mill Lane, and on Saturday mornings (yes, we worked on Saturday mornings), the Junior, "Bimbo", would always sprint to Rima's for a tasty cake or bun, to accompany our morning coffee break.

I should mention that during the War some Canadian soldiers happened to stroll down Mill Lane and look through the Show Room window and were courteously invited inside. This meeting led to an outing to the theatre for some of the staff and soldiers. Later, I corresponded with a very tall lad, nicknamed, "Slim", who came from Manitoba, Canada, and went on to serve in France, before finally returning home.

Looking back, some folk might think that because of its name, Mill Lane was a quiet place, but it was familiar to all and bustled with neighbours, workers and customers, and most folk would nod "Good Morning".

It was a happy environment in which to work.

(Signed)
From: (Miss) Vere E. Smith

Joan Pinfold, the daughter of Fred Whitehouse, also worked in the Mill Lane offices beginning in 1944 as a Junior. She also remembers Miss Kennedy in the Telephone Room, Betty Catton in the Accounts and Mrs. Walker and thinks that Sylvia Bradley was called "Bimbo". There had also been Miss Kelly who had joined the A.T.S.

Just before the end of the War, the first accounts since 1940 were presented to the Directors at their General Meeting on 17th March 1945. Mr Robert Bragg, who was still the Chairman, reported that production had increased by 64% since 1938 with a record output in 1944. Despite big increases in coal, materials and wages, gas prices had only increased by 12% since 1938, well below the average in the country.

With the War in Europe ending in May 1945, and War in the Far East ceasing in the following August, the country began the task of trying to return to some form of normality. Best of all, those men who had been away from the Works for a number of years were able to return, and in particular, Ernie Marshall who had suffered so much was able to come home from Japan. He told me that my father arranged for him to have a full medical check to ensure that he was fully recovered before he began work again. He did recover and returned to his old job as a driver.

On V.E. Day, my father gave instructions for some old gas floodlights to be got out from the stores and Jim Cliffe, with other fitters, went to St. Alphege Church, connected new pipework to the existing supply by one of the buttresses, and installed the floodlights so that the church could be floodlit. Jim remembers the church bells ringing and everyone celebrating outside the George Hotel. Mr. Stephen Downes, who was well liked and had been Manager on the Works throughout the War, always under considerable stress, came along to see how work was progressing and brought a supply of beer for the fitters.

Len Allen, the Mains Superintendent, also visited the men and asked them if they would like fish and chips. There was obviously great support for this idea and Len went down to Billingham's fish and chip shop in the High Street, bought the necessary portions, and the fitters and Len then sat down on the gravestones and celebrated.

The fitters had to make sure the air valves were closed to avoid all the big gas mantles being "blown" which would have incurred the wrath of Mr. Bennett back at the Yard and the floodlights were then lit for two or three nights. I have no idea how long the floodlights remained in action but they were lit again on V.J. Day.

In the following year on 23rd March 1946, Chairman Robert Bragg said that all through the War, the Company had been able to maintain gas at all times and thanked employees and staff for their services in circumstances of difficulty and danger ending with further tributes to Mr S J Sadler, Manager, and all employees.

It had been another satisfactory year with dividends of 9% per annum on the Consolidated and Preference Shares and 4 1/2% per annum on the redeemable Preference Shares.

It is interesting to see on my father's map which was prepared in 1939, not only all the gas mains that had been laid but new roads and housing developments which the Gas Company expected to take place in years to come so that provisions could be made for future gas needs.

These developments, envisaged in 1939, follow very closely those which have now taken place – no doubt there had been discussions with the Council Surveyor at the time.

During 1946, 1947 and 1948, the number of houses being built gradually increased and the Gas Company began spending quite large amounts on new mains and the number of customers began to rise again.

However, in July 1945, the Labour Party had swept to power and the greatest single event in the history of the gas industry was soon to take place. Nationalisation of many industries had been a major part of the Labour Party policy and the Government were anxious to proceed as soon as they were able.

The Nationalisation programme did not alter the programme of Solihull Gas Company in any way. In 1947, £6,682 was spent on new mains, production increased by 4 million cubic feet and in 1948, £10,180 was spent on new mains.

The Bill for Nationalisation of the Gas Industry came before Parliament and the Gas Act 1948 was entered in the Statute Book. At the last General Meeting of Solihull Gas Company on 19th March 1949, Mr Robert Bragg announced that the Company was to be wound up under Nationalisation on 1st May.

He reported that, since the formation of the Company in 1869, 120 miles of mains had been laid and the total of customers had reached 10,400. He also said that the Board had always realised the great importance of giving customers efficient service and the Company would be handed over to the new West Midlands Gas Board in a sound and efficient order.

The last meeting of the staff and employees of Solihull Gas Company while still under private ownership took place at the Council House in Poplar Road on Friday, 29th April 1949. There were 90 employees at the dinner to mark the occasion with nationalisation commencing the following day.

Mr Robert Bragg JP, Chairman, made a brief speech thanking the men and outlined the new situation. During his 16 years with the Company, he said, he had watched steady progress being made and they would take pride in handing over to the Government a firm, that with up-to-date equipment, was clean and modern. He trusted the employees to keep up their high standard of efficiency, and sincerely hoped that they would all be happy under the new ownership.

Mr S J Sadler, Director, General Manager and Secretary gave details of the history of the Company and said it was shortly to start a new era. It was interesting to note that the price of gas was still the same as it was in 1883.

It appears that "here and there" amongst the employees there had been "expressions of consternation and questions regarding the future conditions" but they "cheered enthusiastically" when my father concluded by saying:

"To my knowledge, no change will take place so far as the employees are concerned. If it is any comfort to you, I shall still be with you and you can rest assured I shall do my best for you." (S.J.S. was in fact to stay until his retirement in 1955).

"I contend that the Solihull Gas Company has always given first class service to the consumer and the undertaking will continue to give that service".

Unfortunately, the gas industry in 1949 was not really aware that they would soon be entering troubled waters and Solihull Gas Works was only going to be in full production for a few more years.

Electricity was becoming more competitive but even more so was the oil industry. In addition, the new National Coal Board, who took over the whole of the coal industry when it was nationalised, were making big increases in the price of coking coal which was the raw material of the gas industry and so gas prices had to go up. The Coal Board may have thought that they had captive purchasers in the new regional Gas Boards but, if so, they were soon to learn otherwise.

The new Gas Council decided they must look into other means of producing gas, other than by coal, and in 1950 it was decided that a new Research Station must be built in the Midlands. The site chosen was in Wharf Lane, Solihull, behind the houses in Cornyx Lane and Alston Road, and it was rather ironic that the new Research Station, which in due course would be partly responsible for closing all the old gas works using coal, should be built on land purchased by Solihull Gas Company in 1938 for £1,800 ready for their own expansion.

The new Midland Research Station's first building was opened in 1955. The building was called the "Davy Building" and staff were transferred from other research centres in Poole and Beckenham. Research began into various ways of producing gas from petroleum products and in particular, the use of gas in industry.

Another method of producing gas being pursued at that time was by the "Lurgi" process and it was decided to build a big new plant at Coleshill. There was now a distinct move in the mid 1950's away from coal based gas as ever higher coal prices meant that gas became uncompetitive.

In the late 1940's, gas engineers genuinely thought that their methods of production were efficient and in Solihull they had a modern Works; after all the latest Retort House had only been built in 1941. Very few people including all those at a meeting of the Midland Association of Gas Engineers, see Fig. 23, could at that time have envisaged the rapid changes in technology, new chemical products, high coal prices and above all in due course, the discovery of colossal quantities of natural gas under the North Sea.

In addition, gas works did not offer very pleasant working conditions and when all the factors were added up, almost every gas works in the country would soon be obsolete. Even the Lurgi plant at Coleshill never went into full production and it was closed in 1969, so fast was the industry changing.

In 1959, the first large quantities of liquefied gas began to be imported but more importantly by far in that year, was the first and almost unexpected finding of natural gas in huge amounts in Holland. However, because of the legal problems regarding exploration in the North Sea, it was not until 1965 that the existence of further massive quantities of natural gas was confirmed.

The discovery of liquefied gas and then natural gas sounded the death knell of all gas works, including of course, Solihull Works. The West Midlands Gas Board were well aware of these fundamental changes and at that time were looking for somewhere to build their new Headquarters. There was no need to look any further than Wharf Lane, Solihull. The Gas Works would be closing anyway and so why not do it straightaway and this would release a large area of land suitable for development. Solihull was, and still is, a very pleasant place in which to live and work and the Headquarters would also be next door to the Midland Research Station which was growing all the time and in due course, by the 1970's, covered 10 acres of land and employed 400 people.

There was sufficient land available for the new office building, in the first phase, without interfering with the actual Gas Works except for one gasholder and the Foreman's house which had to be demolished to make way for construction to start. I understood that

Fig. 23 A meeting of the Midland Association of Gas Engineers

Fred Snow, the Foreman, then moved to Clacton-on-Sea and started making "seaside rock" instead of gas! On his retirement, Fred was presented with a bicycle and in fact once returned to Solihull, riding his new bicycle from Clacton – there and back – not a bad performance.

I am not quite sure when Solihull Gas Works ceased production but in early June 1962 I heard that the Works was closing so I went to have a look and take photographs and found in fact that the Works had already closed, see Fig 21.

Fig. 24. The West Midlands Gas Board Headquarters in course of construction in 1962 and our family house shortly before demolition

The new Headquarters building can be seen in the course of construction behind our old house (Fig. 24) which was very soon to be demolished together with the original Works Offices and with the garden that still remained, a new car park could then be made.

The new Board Headquarters (Fig. 25), I believe the largest single storey "open plan" office building in Europe at that time, was opened on 20th October 1962 by Mrs C Harold Leach, wife of the Chairman of the Board.

*Fig. 25. The new Headquarters building on completion in 1962
with Moat Lane in the foreground. The largest gasholder and one
of the smaller gasholders still remain together with Retort House,
Purifier building and the office block. The Manager's House has been
demolished and replaced with a car park. The Midlands Electricity
Board Depot is in front of the Headquarters and the Council Moat Lane
Depot is being built on the left. Development on the Damsonwood
Estate had not begun. Part of the British Gas Midland Research Station
can be seen on the right of the Headquarters.*

81

Jim Cliffe tells me that he and two or three other fitters worked eight hours every day, seven days a week for 6 months installing all the piping, most of it in underfloor ducts, such was the rush to complete the building.

The other aerial photograph, see Fig. 26, shows the Works and new Headquarters building from the opposite angle with the canal in the foreground. The rural scene round Solihull Gas Works in 1936 had somewhat altered in 26 years although the Solihull By-pass had not been built.

It can also be seen that the Anchor Inn had been demolished. Ernie Marshall told me that it was one of his last jobs to help with the demolition of the inn but they were able to save the block of stone which had been built into the front wall which had an anchor carved into it. The stone weighed 4 cwt and he heard later that it had been taken to somebody in Damson Lane but that seems to be the last trace of it, which is a pity.

Shortly afterwards, the whole of the Gas Works, except for the two remaining gasholders, was demolished and it was not long before even the holders were cleared away to make further room for expansion of the Board Headquarters and a very large car park.

Coincidentally, it was also in 1962 that Solihull Borough Council received approval for the re-development of Solihull Town Centre and work soon began on the demolition of the whole of Mill Lane and Drury Lane together with all the old properties between High Street and Warwick Road, including of course the Gas Showroom and Offices.

Fig. 26. A view of the new Headquarters building in 1962 and remaining buildings of the old Gas Works, shortly to be demolished, with the canal in the foreground. The line of Wharf Lane still remains but the Anchor Inn has also been cleared away. The British Gas Research Station is to the left of Wharf Lane and in front of Alston Road. Lode Lane is on the right with the Vulcan Road Estate but the Solihull By-pass had not been started.

Fig. 27. Cottages in Mill Lane being demolished with the corner of the Gas Showrooms and offices on the left

For me, the closure of the Gas Works and premises in Mill Lane in 1962 and the clearing away of so much of the old "Village" marked the end of an era and another page had been turned in Solihull's History Book. Perhaps it would be a nice idea to have a suitable plaque displayed in the present Gas Showroom in Mill Lane to record the old Showroom which had been in the same spot and also the existence of the Gas Works in Wharf Lane – I must have a word with British Gas!